# 1 MONTH OF
# FREE
# READING

at

## www.ForgottenBooks.com

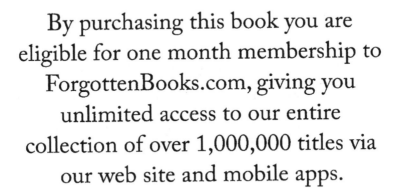

By purchasing this book you are eligible for one month membership to ForgottenBooks.com, giving you unlimited access to our entire collection of over 1,000,000 titles via our web site and mobile apps.

To claim your free month visit:

www.forgottenbooks.com/free922455

ISBN 978-0-260-01703-1
PIBN 10922455

# MINUTES

### OF THE

# ⊰ORGANIZATION⊱

### OF THE

# Liberty Baptist Association,

### AT

## Mt. Tabor M. H., Randolph County, N. C.,

*SEPTEMBER 24th, 1832.*

—ALSO—

## Of the First Session

### HELD AT

## Jamestown Guilford County, N. C.

*17, 18, and 19, of NOVEMBER, 1892.*

3

# MINUTES

## Of the Organization of the Liberty Baptist Association.

Minutes of the Liberty Association convened at Mount Tabor Meeting House, Randolph county, N. C., on the 24th day of September, A. D., 1832.

After prayer by Elder Jesse Sowell.

On motion William Burch was appointed Moderator, and Bro. Peter Owen, Clerk.

A committee was appointed consisting of Elders John Culpepper, William Burch and brother Peter Owen to draft the reasons of the split in the Abbott's Creek Union Association.

Letters from the different churches called for and read. Messengers names enrolled and their state minuted as follows:

| CHURCHES. | MESSENGER'S NAMES. | Numbers. | Contributions. |
|---|---|---|---|
| Lick Creek, | Elder Eli Carroll, John Adderton. and Jacob Goss, | 11 | $1.00 |
| Jersey Settlement | Josiah Wiseman, George and Humphrey Owen, | 68 | .60 |
| Abbott's Creek, | William Raper. Alex. Thomas and Davis Raper, | 13 | .50 |
| Tom's Creek, | Elder Jesse Sowell, James Brown and Benj. Lanier, | 16 | .75 |
| Jamestown, | Elder Wm. Burch, Isaac Beeson and David Idol, | 9 | .50 |
| Liberty, | Peter Owen, Joshua Lee and Philip Copple, | 27 | 1 25 |
| Holloway's, | Thomas Hatcher and Christopher Hedrick: | 15 | .80 |
| TOTAL, | | 159 | $5.40 |

1ST. This Association shall be called the Liberty Association.

2ND. Called for corresponding messengers: Elders Eli.Philips and Lane Hudson from Sandy Creek with minutes: Elder John Culpepper from Pedee with minutes being rejected by the majority was received by us.

3RD. Appointed a Committee or Finance, brethren Raper and Lanier.

4TH. Corresponding Messengers appointed to the following Associations: To the Yadkin, Elder Carroll and Peter Owen; To the Pedee, Benjamin Lanier and John Adderton; To Sandy Creek, Elder William Burch and Davis Raper; To the Raleigh, Elder Jesse Sowell and James Brown; To the Cape Fear, Elder Jesse Sowell and Josiah Wiseman.

5TH. The Committee appointed to draft the reasons of the division in the Abbott's Creek Union Association reported and their report received and ordered to be annexed to these minutes.

6TH. The Committee of Finance reported six dollars and forty cents contributed by the churches.

7TH. Our next Association to be at Jamestown on the Saturday before the third Lord's day in November next. Elder Eli Carroll appointed to preach the introductory sermon and in case of failure, Elder Jesse Sowell.

8TH. Appointed Davis Raper to superintend the printing of these minutes.

The Association rose   Prayer by Elder Burch.

PETER OWEN,                                 ELDER WILLIAM BURCH,
           Clerk.                                          Moderator.

NOTE:—The foregoing record tells of the organization of the Liberty Association. It was a part of the Abbott's Creek Union Association (now anti-missionary.)

There were a great many churches and several Associations that have been missionary in spirit ever since their organization; which was long before the "split" and they never divided. But in the Abbott's Creek Union, those favoring missions, Sunday Schools, etc., were in the minority. And so in the Association in 1832, they were ruled out and went out (says Elder B. Lanier who was present) into a large tent and organized.   H. S.

## MINUTES

*Of the Liberty Association Convened at Jamestown, Guilford County, N. C., on the 17th, 18th and 19th Days of November, 1832.*

### SATURDAY, NOVEMBER 17TH, 1832.

1ST. The Association sermon was delivered by brother George W. Parifoy from the 1st Epistle of Peter 4th chapter, 18 verse: "And if the righteous scarcely be saved, where shall the ungodly and the sinner appear."

2ND. After sermon the Association convened, Elder Burch prayed at the opening of business.

3RD. Letters from the several churches were called for and read. Members names enrolled and their state minuted as follows:

| CHURCHES. | MESSENGERS' NAMES. | Baptized. | Received. | Dismissed. | Restored. | Excommunicated. | Dead. | Numbers. | Contributions. |
|---|---|---|---|---|---|---|---|---|---|
| LICK CREEK, | Elder Eli Carroll, John Parks and Dempsy Parks. | 13 | 0 | 0 | 0 | 0 | 1 | 34 | $ .97½ |
| JERSEY SETTLEMENT, | Josiah Wiseman, Humphrey Owen, Richard Owen. | 5 | 0 | 2 | 0 | 0 | 1 | 68 | 1.15 |
| ABBOTT'S CREEK, | Alex. Thomas, Joseph Spurgeon, Wm. Raper. | 3 | 1 | 0 | 1 | 1 | 0 | 18 | 1.57½ |
| TOM'S CREEK, | Elder Jesse Sowell, Benj. Lanier, James Brown. | 0 | 0 | 1 | 0 | 0 | 0 | 15 | 1.20 |
| JAMESTOWN, | Elder Wm. Burch, Isaac Beeson, David Idol. | 0 | 0 | 0 | 0 | 0 | 0 | 09 | 1.25 |
| LIBERTY, | Peter Owen, John Fine, Wm. Owen. | 0 | 0 | 0 | 0 | 0 | 0 | 27 | 1.50 |
| HOLLOWAY'S, | Christopher Headrick, Thos. Hatcher, | 2 | 1 | 0 | 0 | 0 | 0 | 17 | .50 |
|  | A friend to Zion contributed, |  |  |  |  |  |  |  | .25 |
|  | A friend to Zion contributed, |  |  |  |  |  |  |  | .25 |
|  |  | 23 | 2 | 3 | 1 | 1 0 | 2 | 188 | $8.60 |

4TH. Elected by ballot, William Burch Moderator and Peter Owen, Clerk.

5th. Corresponding Messengers: From the Yadkin Association, Paul Phifer; from the Raleigh Association, George W. Purifoy; from the Sandy Creek Association, Levi Anders, James Hedden and David Patterson.

6TH. Invited ministering brethren to sit with us.

7TH. Elected by ballot Paul Phifer, George W. Purifoy, and Jesse Sowell to preach to-morrow—worship to commence at 11 o'clock.

8TH. Appointed a select committee, consisting of Paul Phifer, George W. Purifoy, Josiah Wiseman, Eli Carroll and Isaac Beeson with the Moderator and Clerk to arrange the business of the Association and prepare a Constitution and Rules of Decorum for the government of the same and report on Monday.

9TH. Committee of Finance: Joseph Spurgeon and James Brown.

10TH. After prayer by Levi Anders, adjourned until Monday morning 10 o'clock.

MONDAY, NOVEMBER 19TH, 1832.

11TH. Met pursuant to adjournment. prayer by Eli Carroll. Proceeded to business.

12TH. Committee of Arrangements reported and presented the following Constitution and Rules of Decorum for the government of this Association when in session which were read and adopted and ordered to be printed with these minutes and Committee discharged.

13TH. Committee of Finance reported that they found in the hands of Joseph Spurgeon $1.90; received from the churches $8.25; from individuals 45 cents; total $10.60. Report received and Committee discharged.

14TH. Called on Corresponding Messengers to report. Report satisfactory.

15TH. The circular letter dispensed with in consequence of the Constitution and Rules of Decorum being attached to these minutes.

16TH. Appointed Peter Owen to prepare a circular to be attached to next minutes.

17TH. Appointed Corresponding Messengers to the following

Associations: To the Yadkin, Josiah Wiseman and Joseph Spurgeon; to Pedee, Joseph Spurgeon and Benjamin Lanier; to Sandy Creek, William Burch and Isaac Beeson; to Raleigh, Jesse Sowell and James Brown; to Country Line, William Burch and David Idol; to Brier Creek, Jesse Sowell and Peter Owen; to to Tar River, Jesse Sowell and James Brown.

18TH Appointed Peter Owen to superintend the printing of these minutes, 400 copies in number and distribute them among the churches of this Union.

19TH. Appointed the next Association at Holloway's meeting house, Davidson commence Saturday before the second Lord's day in November next. Our Associations to be held after the one above named commencing Saturday before the 2nd Lord's day in August in each yea.r Josiah Wiseman to preach the introductory sermon, Jesse Sowell his alternate,

20TH. Appointed communion meetings at the following places: at Abbott's Creek commencing Friday before the third Lord's day in May next. At Tom's Creek, Friday before the first Lord's day in March next. At Jersey Settlement commencing Friday before the third Lord's day in July next. At Liberty commencing Friday before the second Lord's day in August next. And we earnestly solicit our brethren and sisters to endeavor generally to attend these meetings; and especially ministering brethren and exhorters.

21ST. Appointed Peter Owen, Treasurer.

22ND. Resolved, That the Clerk purchase an Association book and transcribe all the proceedings of this Association from its commencement and report to us at our next Association and we pay him for his labor.

23RD. This Association unanimously present this neighborhood with their thanks for the kindness, hospitality and respect with which its members and friends have been treated ever since the commencement of the meeting.

24TH. After an impressive exhortation by George W. Purifoy, the meeting of the Association was closed by singing, and prayer by George W. Purifoy.

PETER OWEN,                                    WILLIAM BURCH,
      Clerk.                                    Moderator.

NOTE :—In the organization of this Association, a Committee

of three, consisting of John Culpepper, Wm. Burch and Peter Owen, was appointed to draft the reasons of the "split."

The reasons were presented in MS. and "received and ordered to be annexed to the minutes." But the record of the organization and of the first session held at Jamestown, N. C., were never printed. And hence, in order to preserve these records from oblivion, they are hereby printed. The reasons of the "split" or division between the Baptists as reported to the Association, were much enlarged by the addition of some most interesting and valuable history.

The Reasons of the split are appended hereto.

HENRY SHEETS.

# THE REASONS OF THE SPLIT.

## The Ministers and Messengers, Composing the Liberty Baptist Association, to the Churches They Represent.

DEAR BRETHREN:—The subject on which we address you at this time, is the origin and history of our own body; in order to give you a correct history of the origin, the rise and progress of our Association, we must resort to the history of the Sandy Creek Association; of which we were a component part, until that body was divided, and we were attached to the southern division of it, which was called the Pee Dee Association; and also a brief history of the Pee Dee Association, until 1815, when the Sandy Creek and the Pee Dee Associations were sub-divided, and the Abbott's Creek Association, formed of the western parts of the two bodies. The Sandy Creek church, the oldest in the Association, originated in the following manner: Shubal Stearns, a native of Boston, Mass., who after laboring for some time among the Independents, in 1751 embraced Baptist sentiment, and was baptized by Wait Palmer, and ordained the same year in Tolland, Conn. Listening to the instructions of heaven as he esteemed them; conceived himself called upon by the Almighty to move to the westward, to execute a great and extensive work. In 1754 and with a few of his friends, took his leave of New England, and travelled to Berkley in Virginia; and thence to Guilford county, N. C., where he took up his permanent residence. Benedict informs us, as soon as they arrived, they built them a little meeting house, and 16 of them, formed themselves into a church, and chose Shubal Stearns for their pastor, who had for his assistants, Daniel Marshall and Joseph Breed, neither of whom were ordained.

In process of time, some of its inhabitants became converts, and bowed obedience to the Redeemer's sceptre: these uniting their labors with the others, a powerful and extensive work commenced, and Sandy Creek church was soon swelled from 16 to 106 members.

Abbott's Creek church was soon constituted, and Daniel Marshall was chosen their pastor. Benedict says: From Sandy

Creek went the word and great was the company of them who published it.

This church has spread her branches westward, to the great Mississippi, southward as far as Georgia, eastward to the sea and Chesapeake Bay, and northward to the waters of the Potomac.

In the year 1758, a few churches having been constituted, and these having a number of branches, which were fast maturing for churches; Stearns conceived that an association of delegates from all, would have a tendency to forward the great object of their exertions. For this purpose he visited each church and congregation and explained to them his contemplated plan, and induced them to send delegates to his meeting house and in January 1758, an Association was formed, which was called Sandy Creek, and which continues to the present time.

This Association has experienced many vicissitudes of prosperity and adversity, and from this old Association, churches have been raised up which have become component parts of several large and flourishing bodies in several States.

In 1815 at an Association held at Rocky Spring, M. H., commencing the 28th of October, 1815, the Association took into consideration the propriety of dividing the Association into two Associations, and resolved that it be divided, and that all the churches on the south-west side of Deep river, shall compose the new Association, to be known as the Pee Dee.

The said Sandy Creek Association did, at the said session, held at Rocky Spring, resolve to send Robert T. Daniel and Robert Ward. as messengers to the general meeting of Correspondence, and send two dollars. They also appointed Robert T. Daniel, Corresponding Secretary to the Baptist Board of Foreign Missions of the United, (I suppose that States is meant.) Elder Bennett Solomon, reported that he attended the General Meeting of Correspondence according to appointment.

The Association appointed Elders John Culpepper and Bennet Solomon Messengers from the Pee Dee Association, to the General Meeting of Correspondence and we contribute two dollars. They also resolved to pay Elders Culpepper and Solomon, five dollars each, for attending the General Meeting of Correspondence.

The Pee Dee Association, into which most of the churches of our body were arranged by the division, met at Richland M. H.,

Montgomery county, on the 19th, 20th and 21st days of October, 1816; when the introductory sermon was preached by Elder J. Culp pper, and J. Culpepper was chosen Moderator, and William Dowd, Clerk,

They adopted Rules of Decorum for the government of the Association, and being actuated by the same missionary spirit, or zeal for the Lord of Hosts and love for immortal souls which actuated Shubal Stearns and his brethren, and diffused itself through the parent Associations at their first session, resolved to appoint J.Culpepper aCorresponding Secretary to the Baptist Board of Foreign Missions and Messenger to the General Meeting of Correspondence. Like the parent Association, his experienced many vicissitudes of prosperity and adversity, but continued to increase in members and churches, until the year 1825 when the division took place, and the Abbott's Creek Association was formed and since that period she has travelled on nearly as formally, and increased in members until September 1832, when at a session held at Mount Tabor in Ran. olph county, an unfortunate division was affected in the following manner:

After the introductory sermon was delivered, the Messengers retired to the house, when Isaiah Spurgeon took the chair as Moderator. The letters were then called for, and two were presented purporting to be from Lick Creek church; the clerk read the letter from the majority, claiming to be the church in which they named Messengers, and in instructed them not to sit with any persons who were advocates of the Baptist State Convention.

Isaiah Spurgeon then arose and said he was inexperienced in the duties of the chair, and remarked that two letters were presented from Lick Creek, and as it was new to him, he asked advice from such as were more experienced than himself. Elder J. Culpepper proposed for them to receive and read the letters from the undivided churches, and then the Association would be competent and could decide which should be received and the minority, if necessary, may retire. Elder Ashley Swaim and others objected to this course, and after considerable debate, it was decided in the negative.

The Moderator then proposed that the members said to be excluded, should retire to their respective churches, and make their acknowledgements and that the Association appoint a committee to labor with them. William Burch objected to it and the question being taken, was decided in the negative. William Spurgeon then proposed that the Association should advise, and the churches call for help and labor with the divided churches and try to bring about a reconciliation. Ashley Swaim, Solomon Snider, Philip Snider and others objected to the proposition, which was rejected.

The Rules of Decorum were then called for and after they were read, Ashley Swaim said the last rule forbid the Association to interfere with the affairs of an independent church and stated that from Eli Carroll's acknowledgement, it was evident that he, and the members which stood with him, had withdrawn from the church, and the church should be received.

Eli Carroll said the majority had declared all who held with the Bible Societies, the Missionary Society or the Sabbath School, were out of their fellowship, and they withdrew, to avoid being excluded. J. Culpepper said he rejoiced that the subject had assumed a tangible shape, so that if the minority had to retire, it could be distinctly ascertained on what grounds we were induced to retire.

The N. C. Baptist State Convention had been frequently named and objected to.

J. Culpepper explained the objects of the Convention to be first to encourage itinerant preaching and supply the destitute churches in our State with preaching. Secondly, to afford assistance to our Baptist brethren in Birmah and help them to supply the Birmans who were applying to them for directions how to escape an eternal hell and to obtain a knowledge of the eternal God, before they die, with the word of God.

Thirdly, to aid our poor young ministers in the attainment of learning and biblical knowledge. Jesse Sowell said, the ground on which he was disowned by the majority of the Tom's Creek church was, that he had given one dollar to aid the Birman mission and attended the Baptist State Convention and call on the majority to say if they had ever charged him with any immoral conduct.

Isaiah Spurgeon said he had no fellowship with any of these institutions and expressed a hope that all who held with him would proceed. James Brown asked him if in his declaration he designed to include those who held with these institutions? He answered: we can not serve God and Mammon and he who is not for us is against us, and said he could not fellowship any person who held with these institutions.

The question was then put, and decided in the affirmative. Some of the minority said, if they could not sit with any person who held with the Bible Society, the Missionary Society or the Sabbath School, we may retire, and we shall do it with satisfaction.

The majority expressed a hope that we would retire and trouble them no more. We retired, and the majority proceeded to read their Letters and appointed their preachers to the entire exclusion of the minority and the Corresponding Messengers.

When the churches and parts of churches disowned by the majority of the Association, as the last and to them the only remaining resort, formed themselves into an Association called the Liberty Association, which at first numbered but 159 members. They met again at Jamestown, Guilford county, N. C., on the 17th, 18th and 19th of November, 1832, when they numbered 188.

Their next session was held at Holloway's M. H., in Davidson county, on the 9th, 10th and 11th days of November, 1833, when their numbers had increased to 270. Since that period, the good hand of our God, as we trust, has been upon us, and Zion's ends in this part of our Lord's vineyard, has been lengthened, and her stakes strengthened. We have received by baptism 307, and our present number is 570.

------

The above, was reported and incorporated with the minutes of the session held at Abbott's Creek in 1834. Several of our old church records of that date tell us much the same story. While the anti-Mission Baptists were in the majority in this particular Association, there were several Associations that never divided at all. They were missionary before the "split" and continue so to this present time. The Liberty Association is carrying on mission work just as our Baptist brethren did before the anti-mission (or Hard Shell) Baptists split off from us. G. W. Purifoy tells us in his history of the Sandy Creek Association, (page 59) that only about one-fifth of the Baptists left us in the division. The Baptists, commonly known as Missionary, are therefore without the shadow of a doubt, the Old Baptists. Any one at all, who knows anything about the history of the denomination during the period from 1825 to 1835, knows that we are the Trunk and all others have gone out from us.

HENRY SHEETS.

August 29th, 1892.

# MINUTES

OF THE

## ELEVENTH ANNIVERSARY

OF THE

# Liberty Association,

HELD AT

## Lick Creek Meeting-House,

DAVIDSON COUNTY, N. C.

August the 19th and 21st days, 1843.

---

BLUM & SON,
BOOK AND JOB PRINTERS,
SALEM, N. C.
1843.

# MINUTES.

1. The introductory sermon was delivered by Elder B. LANIER, from II Corinthians, 8th chapt. 9th verse; brother Wiseman being absent from inability.

2. The Association was organized by Elder B. LANIER acting as Moderator pro tem.

3. After singing and prayer by brother Lanier, church letters were called for, read, and their contents noted, (see last page.) The Association then proceeded to elect brother Lanier, Moderator.

4. Opened a door for the reception of corresponding messengers: Wm. H. Hamner, from the Yadkin; brother R. Jacks from the Brier Creek; and B. H. Carter from the Pee Dee Association;—all with Minutes.

5. Invitation given to ministers, if any present, who are not delegates, to sit with us; brother Eli Philips, from Sandy Creek Association, received the invitation; also brother Carrel and brother Jones.

6. Moved by brother Spurgin and seconded, that we appoint our committees out of our own body, with the leave to call on our corresponding brethren to sit with them.

7. Appointed brethren Spurgin, J. Wiseman and Turner, with the Moderator and Clerk, a Committee of Arrangement.

8. Appointed brethren Abram Palmer and John Teague, a Committee of Finance.

9. Called for the Circular prepared by brother William Turner and referred it to the Committee of Arrangement for inspection.

10. Appointed by ballot, Elders Eli Philips, Richard Jacks and B. H. Carter, to fill the Stand to-morrow. Worship to commence at 10 o'clock.

11. Appointed brother Richard Jacks to preach at 12 o'clock to-morrow;—also a collection to be taken up for home missions.

12. Adjourned until 9 o'clock Monday morning. Prayer by Elder R. Jacks.

# MONDAY, AUGUST 21, 1843.

Met according to adjournment. Prayer by brother Z. Minor.

1. Called over the delegates names, and read the rules of decorum.

2. The Committee of Arrangement reported and were discharged.

3. The Committee of Finance reported that they had received from the churches ten dollars and ninety-six cents; and sixty cents from the Treasurer, making in all eleven dollars and fifty-six cents. Money paid over to the Treasurer, and Committee discharged.

4. Corresponding Messengers reported: Brother Wm. Turner gave satisfactory excuse, and was accordingly excused. Brother Lanier attended the Yadkin Association and was cordially received; brother Charles attended the Brier Creek Association and was received; brother Wiseman failed from inability, and was excused; brother A. Kinney gave a satisfactory excuse for not attending the Pee Dee Association; brother Lanier attended and was received cordially; brother John Teague gave his excuse for not attending the Sandy Creek Association and was excused: The other brethren not present.

5. Appointed corresponding messengers to the following Associations: To the Yadkin Association, to be held the last Saturday in September, brother Josiah Wiseman and brother R. Barnes; to the Brier Creek Association, to be held Saturday before the fourth Sunday in September, in Wilkes county, about 12 miles north from Jonesville, and near the north east corner of Wilkes, brother William Turner and brother Richard Weathering; to the Pee Dee, to be held on Friday before the second Sabbath in October, at Springhill church, Richmond county, N. C., about a mile west of Gilchrist bridge, brother Alfred Kinney and Eli Coggin; to Sandy Creek, to commence on Friday before the fourth Sabbath in September, to be held at Antioch church, Orange county, N. C., brother Z. Miner and John Teague, to attend the same.

6. The circular letter, which was prepared by brother William Turner, was read and unanimously adopted.

7. Appointed brother Azariah Williams to write the next circular letter.

8. Appointed the next Association to be held at Abbott's Creek Church, Davidson county, near Browntown; to commence the Saturday before the third Lord's Day, in August, 1844.

9. Brother William Turner to preach the introductory sermon, and brother A. Kinney, his alternate.

10. Brother Lanier reported that himself and Samuel P. Moten, ordained brother Alfred Kinney, on the fifth Sunday in April last.

11. Agreed by this Association, that we continue the Minister's and Deacon's meeting another year, and that the churches request their officers to attend regular, and report the business of the same to their churches; and we appoint the next meeting to be held at New-Friendship, the fifth Sabbath in next October, with the Saturday before.

11. *Resolved*, That the thanks of this Association be recorded on the minutes to the brethren and friends for their hospitality in supporting this meeting.

12. We find the contributions of the churches to be insufficient to defray the expenses of printing the Minutes, and the Association had to contribute one dollar and forty-four cents for the same.

13. The Missionary sermon was preached by brother Jacks on Monday, instead of Sunday, from Matthew 6th chapter, first clause of the 10th verse. " Thy kingdom come." And a collection taken up immediately for home missions, amounting to sixteen dollars and thirty-one cents.

14. We agree to send one delegate to our Baptist State Convention of North Carolina, to be held at B. S. Camp-ground, Henderson county, N. C., and appoint brother R. Jacks to bear said collection from this Association to the Convention.

BENJAMIN LANIER, *Moderator.*
AZARIAH WILLIAMS, *Clerk.*

# CIRCULAR.

DEAR BRETHREN : We make our present ignorance of the ways of God the subject of this letter. The Providence of God towards us, in many instances, appears mysterious and unintelligible. The truth of this observation will not be called into question; that human affairs are not left to roll on according to mere chance, but that God interposes to some degree, is very plain. When we attempt to trace the conduct of God towards his creatures, our minds are confused, in consequence of its appearing that he does not confine his operations to any definite means to effect his purposes; when, in our meditations, we contemplate the administration of heaven, an unaccountable mixture of apparent order and disorder presents itself to the mind. At one view, we think we see the hand of Providence regulating our affairs to the advancement of our interest and happiness; when suddenly we are disappointed, and our hopes are crossed; where we looked for order nothing but disorder appears. Notwithstanding such an apparent confused state of things, God especially interposes his divine authority, in approbation of the conduct of his followers, and in covering sinners with shame and confusion. But this world is not the place where God's people are to expect to receive their reward. Here we see the humble followers of Christ oppressed, afflicted, cast down and set at naught by mankind; we hear the lamentations of the oppressed on every hand; we meet with weeping parents and mourning friends; we behold the young cut off in the midst of their days, and the aged left desolate, overburdened with affliction and sorrows; while on the other hand we see many of the wicked in affluent circumstances, promoted to honours and distinctions in life, where it appears that nothing can hinder the enjoyment of ease and pleasure; how far from corresponding with the idea which we form of justice does such a state of things appear! When we examine the constitution of the human mind, we discern evident marks of its being framed with a view to approve and reward virtue; and when we appeal to experience we know that our conscience reproved us when we were sinners, and justifies in laboring for Christ. In our present capacity, we need not be surprised that the conduct of God appears mysterious. To us no more than the beginning of things are visible; we trace but a few links of that chain of being, which binds together the present and the future. "As for man his days are as grass; as a flower of the field, so he flourisheth. For the wind passeth over it, and it is gone; and the place thereof shall know it no more." Psalms 103, 15 16.

If a peasant be incapable of judging of the administration of the government of a mighty empire, why should we think it strange that mankind should be at a loss concerning the dealings of God with his rational creatures. We need not expect that complete knowledge of the ways of God will be communicated to us here; for we believe that it would prove a snare, if granted to us in our present state; it would be inconsistent with that state, with the actions we have to perform and the duties we have to fulfil. We are placed here under trial of our virtue; and we have just understanding sufficient to strengthen our faith, and enable us to persevere in our christian course. Had complete information been communicated to us, respecting the ways of God, it would not be for our advantage; our ignorance of future events in relation to ourselves necessarily brings us into a state of trial. In order to exercise our intellectual and moral faculties, we must be left to find our way through the numerous perplexities and disappointments with which we meet: by the perpetual recurrence of these trials, we are strengthened and in some respect fortified against their frequent inroads, and enabled to fill our respective stations with constancy. Had we enjoyed no evidence of a just judge ruling the earth, and of his providence interposing in our affairs, virtue would have been altogether deprived of its encouragement and support; had the evidence on the other hand been so strong as to place the hand of the Almighty constantly before our eyes, virtue would have met with no trial. We are often impatient when our designs do not succeed according to our wishes; ignorant as to what futurity is to bring forward, occupied with nothing but the present, we exclaim, where is God! "Hath he forgotten to be gracious?" Our present can be no other than a state of twilight or dawn, in which we shall find ourselves in a middle condition, between light and darkness, exposed to dangers of every form, surrounded by trials and afflictions of various kinds.— These circumstances often discourage us and furnish cause for heaviness, and wring from us tears of oppression, and make us sigh for deliverance. Though these things may seem mysterious to us at present, the Almighty looks not merely to what we suffer, but what the effect of these sufferings is to be. Our Saviour saith, "What I do thou knowest not now; but thou shalt know hereafter!" Consider in how different a light the patriarch Joseph viewed the events of his life, after he had seen in what they terminated, from the light in which he saw them when led away by the Ishmaelites as a slave, or when thrown by Potipher into prison. When he made himself known to his brethren he said, "Now therefore be not grieved nor angry with yourselves that ye sold me hither, for God did send me before you to preserve life. So now it was not you that sent me hither but God." Genesis 45—5 8. What a wonderful display of the deepest sense of gratitude to God in the conduct of this excellent man! his behaviour evinced the sincerity of his heart in the midst of the severest temptations and trials. It appears that we often have to drink deeply of the bitter cup of suffering. No christian has ever lived without having to partake of many of the sufferings that are incident to human life; nor is the sinner free from such suffering; but christians have trials that sinners know nothing about. "God does not willingly afflict the children of men." Although sufferings and trials appear to be the common lot of man, yet many of the difficulties that assail us arise from our own misconduct or neglect of duty. Consider what David suffered on account of his conduct towards Uriah: The Lord, by the mouth of the prophet Nathan saith: "Now therefore, the sword shall never depart from thy house. Thus saith the Lord, behold, I will raise up evil against thee out of thine own house." 2 Samuel 12—10 11. Consider the difficulties with which the prophet Jonah and his fellow mariners had to encounter, in consequence of his neglect of duty.

The chief misfortunes that befall us in life can be traced to some misconduct of our own. In meditating upon the subject under consideration, we are taught the important lesson, that it is our duty to persevere in the divine life, and meet the difficulties that are to try us, with fortitude and firmness. We should not shrink from the discharge of our duty, when our sun appears to be clouded; they who expect to live always in the enjoyment of the sweet influence of the spirit, will find themselves mistaken; and they who think that we can be in the possession of religion and never feel the tendering emotion of the spirit, are equally mistaken. Religion does not consist of feeling any more than it can exist without it; they who become remiss in the discharge of their duties, when they do not feel the spirit sweetly leading them to it, prove untrue to their trust, and lay a bad example before the world. Such inconstancy has destroyed the influence of many christians, that otherwise might have been useful members of society; it has laid the foundation for many erroneous opinions; it has been the most powerful weapon in the hands of the enemy in effecting his malicious schemes against the church of Christ; it has been the cause, in a great measure, of our ecclesiastical matters being reduced to such a lamentable condition: When we look abroad, we behold, with the mental eye, six hundred millions of the human family who are still destitute of the means of religious instruction! We hear the continual calls of our missionary brethren, who are gone to preach to them, for assistance; we hear that our treasury is exhausted, and that such assistance is not afforded to enable them to carry on their important operations. And when we contemplate the state of things, as it exists at home, we see the great necessity of supporting the Gospel among our own destitute fellow citizens; we see many of them growing up without the means of religious instruction. Such a state of things calls loud for the constant and united efforts of christians! When our spirits are revived, it appears that there is no sacrifice but that we are willing to make: our time, our talents, and our donations are offered up freely. But when our sky appears to be clouded, we sink into indifference; our zeal becomes languid, our minds soon become occupied with the things of the world, and matters of small moment assume the appearance of important things! This should not be the case. We should implore the direction of Heaven, deny ourselves, take up our cross and follow Christ. If we permit ourselves to be drawn away by the charms of the world, and do not strictly conform to the principles of the christian religion, we plunge ourselves into many sorrows; and by such inconstancy, we give occasion for the scoffer to speak reproachfully of us, and of the cause of Christ.

May God, in his infinite mercy, grant us persevering grace, and keep us from the evils of the world; may he grant us the guidance and the tuition of his Holy Spirit, that our path may be as the shining light that shineth more and more unto the perfect day. AMEN.

WILLIAM TURNER.

# A TABLE OF CONTENTS.

| CHURCHES. | COUNTIES. | POST OFFICES. | BY WHOM SUP. PLIED. | DELEGATES' NAMES. | Baptized | Rec'd by Letter | Restored | Dismissed | Excluded | Deceased | Total Number | Contributions | Ch'ch Meetings |
|---|---|---|---|---|---|---|---|---|---|---|---|---|---|
| Lick Creek, | Davidson, | Jackson Hill, | A. Kinney, | A Miller, A Kinney M Redwine | 2 | 1 | | | 3 | 2 | 50 | $1 35 | 4S |
| Jersey, | do | Cotton Grove, | J. Wiseman, | W. Turner, J. Fuzer, J Wiseman | | | | | 1 | 6 | 198 | 2 50 | 1S |
| Abbot's Creek, | do | Browntown, | B. Lanier, | J. Spurgin, D. Raper, J. Teague | | | | | 1 | | 22 | 1 00 | 3S |
| Tom's Creek, | do | Mt. Lebanon, | B. Lanier, | M. Skein, J. Lanier, G. Riley, | 2 | | | 2 | | 1 | 24 | 1 00 | 1S |
| Jamestown, | Guilford, | Jamestown, | No supply | | | | | | | 1 | 8 | | |
| Liberty, | Davidson, | Far Grove, | B. Lanier, | Z. Minor, R. Beckerdite, J. Fine, | | | | 2 | | 2 | 20 | 59 | 2S |
| Holloways, | do | Cotton Grove, | A. Kinney, | C. Smith, G. Cross, A. Palmer, | | | | 1 | | 1 | 78 | 2 25 | 2S |
| New Friendship, | Stokes, | Salem, | No supply | | | | | | | | 13 | | 1S |
| Big Creek, | Montgomery, | Windhill, | S. P. Moton, | Mathew Davis, Eli Davis, | | 2 | | | 1 | 1 | 20 | 50 | 3S |
| Pine M. House, | Davidson, | Jersey Settlement, | J. Wiseman, | E. Nunly, R. Barnes, J. Hunt, | | | | 1 | 1 | 1 | 12 | 82 | 4S |
| Reed's X Roads, | do | Lexington, | W. H. Hanner, | A. Williams, B Myers, A. Yarbrough, A. Craver, | 14 | | | 9 | | 2 | 53 | 72 | 2S |
| Marion, | do | | P. Owen, | R. Weatherington, W. Owen, A. Weatherington, | 5 | | | | | | 54 | 25 | 4S |
| | | | | | 21 | 3 | | 13 | 4 | 19 | 552 | 10 96 | |

This Association has within its bounds four ordained preachers, to wit: Eli Carrel and A. Kinney, of Lick Creek; J. Wiseman, of Jersey; and B. Lanier, of Tom's Creek. And Licentiates six in number, viz: William Turner, of Jersey; J. R. Owen and H. McAlpen, of Marion; Z. Minor, of Liberty; A. Williams, of Reed's X Roads; and Dempsey Parks, of Lick Creek.

# MINUTES

## OF THE THIRTEENTH ANNIVERSARY OF THE

### *LIBERTY ASSOCIATION,*

*Held at Jersey Church, Davidson Co., N. C., August* 16,18, 1845.

---

1. The introductory sermon was delivered by br. A. KINNEY, from II Cor. 5th chapter, 20th verse.

2. The Association was then organized by br. W. H. HAMNER acting as Moderator *pro tem.*, and br. N. PARKS, Clerk *pro tem.*

3. After singing and prayer by br. McNabb, letters from the Churches were handed in, and their contents noted. (See last page.) The Association then proceeded to elect br. ELI CARROL, *Moderator.*

4. Opened the doors for the reception of corresponding messengers: Br. P. Phifer and Thompson, from the Yadkin Association, and br. J. J. James, from the Bulah Association, appeared, and were received.

5. An invitation given to ministering brethren to take seats with us: Brethren McNabb, agent for the Wake Forest College, and J. J. James, agent for the Baptist State Convention, br. Wm. H. Hamner and Wm. Turner, accepted the invitation.

6. Appointed brethren James Wiseman, John Charles and Alfred Kinney, with the Moderator and Clerk, a Committee of Arrangements.

7. Appointed brethren Enoch Davis and A. Delappe, a Committee of Finance.

8. Called for the Circular prepared by B. Lanier.

9. Brethren Hamner, Phifer, McNabb, J. J. James and Wm. Turner, appointed a Committee on Church Letters, and State of Religion, and report to this Association on Monday next.

10. The same Committee as in No. 9, instructed to take into consideration the subject of Sabbath Schools and report on Monday next.

11. Appointed Elders P. Phifer, R. McNabb and J. J. James, to occupy the stand on to-morrow. Preaching to commence at 10 o'clock; and br. J. J. James to preach the missionary sermon at 11 o'clock, and a collection to be taken up for Home Missions.

12. Adjourned until Monday 10 o'clock.

## SABBATH.

Elder R. McNabb preached from Jeremiah the 20th ch. and first clause of the 23rd verse. Elder J. J. James followed from Phil. 2nd ch. 5th verse, and preached a missionary sermon. Elder P. Phifer preached from Romans 2nd ch. 4th verse.

## MONDAY, AUGUST 18th, 1845.

Met according to adjournment. Prayer by br. Paul Phifer.

1. Called over delegates' names, and read the rules of decorum.

2. The Committee of Arrangements reported and were discharged.

3. The Committee of Finance reported that they had received from the churches $12 87½ cents. Money paid over to the Treasurer, and committee discharged.

4. Corresponding Messengers reported : Brn. Wm. Turner and N. Parks, appointed to the Yadkin, gave satisfactory cause to the Association. Br. J. Spurgin and David Huffman, attended the Brier Creek Association, and were cordially received. Br. Eli Coggin attended the Pedee Association, instead of the brethren appointed, and was cordially received. Br. Wm. H. Hamner was excused for not attending the Sandy Creek Association ; br. J. Charles attended and was cordially received.

5. Br. Wm. Turner, our delegate to the Convention, reported that he attended the Convention and was received cordially ; paid over the money to the Treasurer, and approved highly of the management of the same.

6. Appointed corresponding messengers to the following Associations : To the *Yadkin* Association, brn. Wm. H. Hamner, Wm. Turner and A. Williams ; to be held at Flat Rock, on Saturday before the first Sunday in October. To the *Brier Creek*, brn. Wm. H. Hamner, A. Delappe and D. Huffman ; to be held on Saturday before the fourth Sabbath in September. To the *Pedee*, brn. A. Kinney, B. Lanier and Eli Coggin ; to be held on Friday before the second Sabbath in October. To the *Sandy Creek*, brn. Wm. Turner, N. Parks and E. Davis ; to be held at the Mineral Springs, Chatham County, commencing on Friday before the fourth Sabbath in September.

7. Appointed Wm. Turner to write the next circular address.

8. Appointed the next Association to be held at Lick Creek church, Davidson County, to commence the Saturday before the third Sabbath in August next.

9. Appointed br. Wm. Turner to preach the introductory sermon ; br. B. Lanier his alternate.

10. A Query was taken up from Reeds Church, which was discussed and laid on the table.

11. The circular letter prepared by br. Lanier, was read and unanimously adopted.

12. The collection taken up for Home Missions, amounted to $17 50 ; and we appoint br. D. Huffman, our delegate to the Baptist State Convention, to bear the same.

13. Called on Committee of Church Letters and the State of Religion, and also of Sabbath Schools, to report : Comittee reported—report received and committee discharged. (See pages 3 and 4.)

14. *Resolved,* That this Association highly approves of the organization of the Southern Baptist Convention for Foreign and Domestic

Missions, and direct that their funds for Foreign Missions, be sent to its Foreign Board, located in Richmond

15. *Resolved*, That a Committee of three be appointed to write a short biographical sketch of the late Elder Josiah Wiseman, and that it be published in our minutes. We accordingly appoint brn. Wm. Turner, B. Lanier and A. Williams, to attend to the same.

16. *Resolved*, That this Association recommend to the churches composing the same, that they delegate to it the power of appointing Presbyteries for the ordination of ministers within its bounds, and that they send up their opinion to the next Association.

17. *Resolved*, That the thanks of this Association be recorded on the minutes, to the brethren and friends for their hospitality in supporting this meeting.

18. We appoint the Clerk to attend to the printing of these Minutes—500 in number.

19. Your Committee on the State of Religion, have nothing interesting to report. Nearly all the letters represent the churches in a cold and lukewarm condition, and as having had very few accessions during the associational year ; scarcely any of them speak favorably of the state of religion among them. Your committee therefore think it should be a subject of serious inquiry as to the causes of such a sad state of things in the present condition of the churches. Why is the Lord withholding his blessings from us ?—Is it because he is unable or unwilling to bless us ?—Certainly not : for his Word assures us that he is more ready to give than we are to receive. The cause then must lie with us : We are either too indifferent to the interest of Zion, or too much engrossed in the world, or are too prayerless, or too unwilling to make sacrifices to have the Word dispensed amongst us.

Your committee feel that the subject committed to them is one of very great importance ; they feel that the present low state of religion, not only in this Association, but throughout the country, calls for a more diligent use of the means of grace.—They think that a time of prayer, both by ministers and churches, should be set apart for outpourings of the Spirit. Your committee would therefore recommend, in view of the present state of religion, that this Association appoint a day of fasting, humiliation and prayer to Almighty God, for a revival of his work amongst us. All of which is respectfully submitted.

PAUL PHIFER, *Chairman.*

20. The Committee on Sabbath Schools beg leave to report, that they are deeply impressed with the utility and importance of these institutions. The future interest of the rising generation depends, in a great degree, upon the moral and religious instruction which they receive in childhood and youth. If children are permitted to grow up ignorant of God's Word and without the wholesome instruction of the S. School, they will be likely to give way to every evil and wicked influence by which they are surrounded. The greatest safeguard

against error is the inculcation of truth; and truth properly taught to the young, seldom fails to make impressions for good, which will continue through life. The most happy results have, in thousands of instances, followed the labors of S. Schools: many who, a few years ago, were S. School scholars, are now, by the grace of God, among the most useful members of the church of Christ. If therefore, as christians, we are anxious to see the children in our respective neighborhoods preserved from wicked associations, from sabbath-breaking, swearing, lying, and every species of evil to which youth is exposed; and if we wish to see them increasing in knowledge of God, growing up prepared to become moral, respectful and useful members of society, let us teach them in the S. School. But S. Schools are not only beneficial to the scholars, but the teachers are often improved in knowledge and grace to a most happy extent. Our S. School teachers are generally the most pious, intelligent and useful members of the church; and, in learning others, they become wiser themselves.

Deep your committee would express their regret, that they have nothing favorable to report in reference to S. Schools within the bounds of this Association; and they are pained to say that there is not, to their knowledge, a single one within its limits. This is a fact we feel deeply to deplore. While the churches are all friendly in sentiment to this department of benevolent effort, they fail to exert themselves to maintain a S. School among them. Your committee can but hope that renewed exertions will be made in each church to establish and maintain them, believing that they will, as instruments, yield much fruit to the honor and glory of God. Your committee recommend also the adoption of the following resolution:

*Resolved,* That the present need of moral and religious instruction to the rising generation amongst us, presents a strong motive for engaging in the work of S. Schools.

All of which is respectfully submitted. J. J. JAMES, *Chairman.*

Adjourned by singing and prayer, by R. McNabb, to the time and place appointed. ELI CARROL, *Moderator.*

AZARIAH WILLIAMS, *Clerk.*

---

## Constitutions of the Churches.

LICK CREEK was constituted by Elders John Culper, Josiah Wiseman and B. Lanier, the 25th of March, 1833:
Number of white members, 41; colored 2; Total 43.

JERSEY CHURCH, the 16th of October, 1784, taken from the minutes with 14 members at that time; by Wm. Sims and Wm. Hill, containing 201 members at present, one-half supposed to be colored.

ABBOTTS' CREEK, in 1832; number of members at present, 30.

TOM'S CREEK, on the 20th of October, 1811:
Number of whites 21; colored 4: Total 25.

JAMESTOWN, not represented.

LIBERTY, the 22d of August, 1829: whites 55; colored 2; Total 57.

HOLLOWAY ; time of constitution not given in letter, but number of members :  whites 47 ; colored 23 :  Total 70.

NEW FRIENDSHIP, in 1826, with 14 members at present—all white.

BIG CREEK; time not given.

PINE MEETING HOUSE; the time of constitution not given in letter.

REED's ⋈ ROADS, on the 12th of October, 1839, by Rev. Josiah Wiseman and Barton Roby, with 25 members at that time, all white.

MARION, August the 1st, 1841, by the Rev. Eli Carrol and B. Lanier, with 44 whites and 2 colored members, at the present.

## Biographical Sketch.

The committee which was appointed to write a biographical sketch of the late Elder JOSIAH WISEMAN, have drawn up the following :

He was born January the 29th, 1783, of respectable christian parents, who brought him up in the fear and admonition of the Lord.—He early became the subject of religious impressions, which increased until he was hopefully converted to God, in the 19th year of his age. He united with the church at Jersey M. H., Rowan County, (now Davidson) N. C., and was baptized the 5th of July, 1812, by Bennet Solomon. Amid the toils and cares of a toilsome life, he remained a pillow in the church and a light to the world. In process of time, he felt that it was his duty to preach the gospel ; he was licensed A. D. 1831, and increased in strength and wisdom, by living in obedience to the divine command: He was ordained February 17th, 1833, by Joseph Pickler, Eli Carroll and Wm. Birch, and was called to the pastoral care of the church at Jersey, at the same time, where he continued to discharge the duties of a Pastor, with the exception of two years, until he died, on the 18th of October, 1844, in the 62d year of his age.

He was dignified in his deportment, possessed a firm, unwavering mind, and was persevering in his undertakings. His manner of preaching was plain, and easy to be understood : " Ye must be born again," was the doctrine upon which he particularly insisted ; and that we merely being the descendants of christian parents, or even of Abraham, are not entitled to church privileges. He was a faithful minister of the gospel ; nothing, but being confined to his bed, prevented him from meeting his appointments, and discharging his christian duties. We regret that we have neither time nor space to write more fully upon the faithfulness of our beloved brother. What language can express the usefulness of such an excellent man ? We fear that we would but shade the light which he so brilliantly reflected. He has gone the way of all the earth ; and his spirit, we fondly hope, is among the spirits of the just made perfect, who, by faith and patience, are now inheriting the promises. But he lives in the hearts of his friends, who think of him with fond regret, and his praise is not only in the church of which he was a member, but in all the churches.

WILLIAM TURNER, *Chairman.*

# Circular Letter.

DEAR BRETHREN :—Permit us, in the present Circular, to call your attention to the duties of Church Members towards each other.

The first, and which indeed seems to include every other, is LOVE. The stress which is laid on this in the Word of God, both as respects the manner in which it is stated and the frequency with which it is enjoined, sufficiently prove its vast importance to the christian temper, and its powerful influence on the communion of believers. It is enforced by our Lord as the identifying law of his kingdom. "This is my commandment, that ye love one another as I have loved you." (John 15 ; 12.) By this we learn that the subjects of Christ are to be known and distinguished amongst men by their mutual affection. This injunction is denominated the new commandment of our Lord. And by the Apostle "Forbearing one another in love." (Eph. 4 : 2.) In a christian church, especially when it is of considerable magnitude, we must expect to find a very great diversity of character. There are all gradations of intellect and all the varieties of temper. In such cases great forbearance is absolutely essential to the preservation of harmony and peace. The strong must bear with the infirmities of the weak. Christians of great attainments in knowledge should not in their hearts despise, nor in their conduct ridicule the feeble conceptions of those who are babes in Christ; but most meekly correct their errors, and most kindly instruct their ignorance. This is love; and such amongst church members, will cultivate peace and harmony, one with another.

Keep the unity of the Spirit in the bonds of peace. (Eph. 4 : 3.) Be of one mind ; live in peace. (II Cor. 3, Rom, 14 : 19.) It is quite needless to expatiate on the value and importance of peace. What societies can exist without it ? I shall therefore proceed to state what things are necessary for the attainment of this end : First, members should be subject one to another in humility ; likewise ye younger, submit yourselves unto the elder. Yea, all of you, be subject one to another, and be clothed with humility. (I Pet. 5 : 5.) Now from hence we learn, that some kind of mutual subjection ought to be established in every christian church. This of course does not mean that some members are to make an entire surrender of their oppinions and feelings to others, so far as never to oppose them, and always be guided by them. It is not the subjection of an inferior to a superior, but of equals to one another; not that which is extorted by authority, but voluntarily conceded by affection ; not yielded as matter of right only, but given for the sake of peace. In short, it is the mutual subjection of love and humility. The democratic principle in our system of church government must not be stretched too far. The idea of equal rights is soon abused and converted into means of turbulence and faction. Liberty, fraternity and equality, are words which, both in church and state, have often become the signals in the mouths of some, for the lawless invasion of the rights of others. It has been strangely forgotten, that no man in social life has a right to please himself only: his will is, or ought to be, the good of the whole. And that individual violates at once the social compact, whether in ecclesiastical or civil society, who pertinaciously and selfishly exclaims, "I will have my way!" Such a declaration constitutes him a rebel against the community. Yet, alas! how much of this rebellion is to be found, not only in the world, but in the church; and what havoc and desolation has it occasioned! Unfortunately for the peace of our societies, it is sometimes disguised by the deceitfulness of the human heart, under the cloak of zeal for the general good. Church members should enter into these sentiments, and thus comply with the apostolic admonitions: "Let nothing be done through strife or vain glory, but, in lowliness of mind, let each esteem others better than themselves. (Phil. 2:3) In honor, prefering one another. (Rom. 12:10.)

Secondly, To the preservation of peace, a right treatment of offences is essentially necessary. We should ever be cautious not to give offence; and we should be as backward to receive offences as we ought to be in giving them. It should be our fixed determination, never, if possible, to occasion a moment's pain. For this purpose, we should be discreet, and mild, and courteous in all our language, weighing the import of words before we utter them, and calculating the consequences of actions before we perform them. We should remember that we are moving in a crowd, and be careful not to trample on or jostle the feelings of our brethren. And when our brother offends us in such a manner, that it becomes our duty to deal with him, we should observe the rule given by our Saviour in the 18th chapter of Matthew. And when it is strictly adhered to, there is no danger of our churches being pestered with many troublesome difficulties. Now if our brother trespass against us, go, said Christ, and tell him his fault between him and thee alone: if he shall hear thee, thou hast gained thy brother. But if he will not hear thee, then take with thee one or two more, that in the mouth of two or three witnesses every word may be established. And if he shall neglect to hear them, tell it unto the church; but if he neglect to hear the church, let him be unto thee as a heathen man and a publican.

Dear brethren, the above direction is so plain that it needs no comment. But observe, tell him his fault alone; not to another, but to him; and if he will not hear thee, then one or more should be called on to aid in trying to make peace. And this all should be done in humility and prayer; and if to no purpose, then tell it to the church. But instead of obeying the advice of the Saviour upon the subject, how often do brethren act to the counter. Dear brethren, in all cases of difference between members of our denomination, let us attend to the direction of Christ, and never tell it to the world. O, may the good Being enable us to obey him in all things, and to serve him faithfully in this world, and finally crown us heirs in Heaven. And all the praise, honor, and glory shall be due unto the Father, Son and Holy Spirit. AMEN.                                                    B. LANIER,

# A Table of Contents.

| CHURCHES | COUNTIES | POST OFFICES | BY WHOM SUPPLIED | DELEGATES' NAMES. | Baptized | Rec'd by Let'r | Restored | Dismissed | Excluded | Deceased | Total Numb'r | Contributions | Ch. Meetings |
|---|---|---|---|---|---|---|---|---|---|---|---|---|---|
| Lick Creek, | Davidson, | Jackson Hill, | A. Kinney, | A Kinney, James Adderton, Michael Fite, | 1 | 1 | | 1 | | 1 | 43 | 1 50 | 4S |
| Jersey, | do | Cotton Grove, | Wm. Turner, | Peter S Miller, Henry Smith, Jas. Wiseman, | | | | | | 10 | 201 | 2 51 | 1S |
| Abbotts' Creek, | do | Browntown, | W H. Hamner | Davis Raper, J Spurgin, John Welch, | | | | | 1 | 1 | 30 | 1 00 | 3S |
| Tom's Creek, | do | Mount Lebanon, | B. Lanier, | B Lanier, George Riley, Wm A Gallimore | | | | 3 | | | 25 | 37½ | 1S |
| Jamestown, | do | No Supply | No Supply | | | | | | | | 8 | | 4S |
| Liberty, | Guilford, | Jamestown, | B. Lanier, | Benj May, John Fine, David Kanoy, | 13 | | | | | | 57 | 1 52 | 2S |
| Holloways, | Davidson, | Fair Grove, | A. Kinney, | George Cross, Chas Smith, F Beanblossom, | 1 | | | | | | 70 | 1 55 | 2S |
| New Friendship | do | Cotton Grove, | No Supply | John Charles, John Styers, Alex Dolappe, | | | | | | | 14 | 75 | 1S |
| Big Creek, | Stokes, | Salem, | S. Moton, | Eli Coggin, Enoch Davis, Wm Crowder, | 6 | | 2 | | | | 28 | 75 | 3S |
| Pine M. H. | Montgomery | Windhill, | No Supply | Elisha Nunnaly, Rich'd Barnes, Jno Hunt, | | | | | | | 12 | 9 00 | 4S |
| Reed's X Roads | Davidson, | Jersey Settlement. | Wm. Turner, | G Tussey, Aaron Yarbrough, J A Parkes, | | | | 3 | 3 | 3 | 53 | 1 25 | 2S |
| Marion, | do | Lexington, | A. Williams | J R Owen, R Witherington, Wm Owen, | | | | 1 | 3 | 1 | 46 | 75 | 4S |
| | | do | | Total, | 21 | 1 | 2 | 6 | 4 | 15 | 589 | 12 87 | |

This Association has within its bounds six Ordained Preachers, to wit: Eli Carrol, A. Kinney and William Turner, of Jersey; Benjamin Lanier, of Tom's Creek; W. H. Hamner and A. Williams, of Reed's X Roads. And four Licentiates: G. Tussey, of Reed's X Roads; J. R. Owen, Hugh McAlpen and Demsey Parkes, of Lick Creek.

# MINUTES

## FIFTEENTH ANNIVERSARY

OF THE

# LIBERTY ASSOCIATION,

HELD AT

## ABBOTT'S CREEK CHURCH,

DAVIDSON COUNTY, N. C., (NEAR BROWNTOWN,)

*August the* 14th *and* 16th *days,* 1847.

---

1. The introductory sermon was delivered by br. W. Turner, (in the absence of A. Williams) from Hebrews 13, 1: "Let brotherly love continue."

2. The Association was then organized by br. B. Lanier acting as Moderator *pro tem.*, and Wm. Turner, Clerk *pro tem.*

3. After singing and prayer by br. B. Lanier, letters from the churches were handed in, and their contents noted. (See last page.) The Association then proceeded to elect br. B. Lanier, Moderator.

4. Opened the doors for the reception of corresponding messengers : br. M. May and N. S. Chaffin, from the Yadkin; J. Oaks, from Bulah, and J. J. James, and also as Agent for Foreign Missions, and delivered a thrilling address on the subject, and took up a collection for the same, amounting to $7 66.

5. An invitation given to ministering transient brethren to take seats with us : Wm. H. Jordan accepted the same.

6. Appointed J. Spurgen, A. Kinney, A. Palmer, with the Moderator and Clerk, a Committee of Arrangements.

7. Appointed br. R. Wetherington and E. H. Davis, a Committee of Finance.

8. Called for Circular. On motion, the Association wait on br. Williams.

9. On motion, called on Committee on the State of Religion and Church Letters to report.

10. On motion, gave until Monday to examine church letters.

11. Called on Committee of Sabbath Schools : Nothing interesting to report.

12. On motion, continued the same committee next year.

13. On motion, agreed that the committee which was appointed (by Abbott's Creek Church) to arrange the preaching during the meeting, be empowered to arrange preaching on the Sabbath.

14. On motion, referred a memorial, presented by W. H. amner, to the Committee of Arrangements.

15. On motion, agreed that a collection be taken on Sabbath, after 11 o'clock sermon, for missionary purposes.

16. On motion, adjourned until Monday 9 o'clock. Prayer by br. M. May.

### SABBATH.

At 9 o'clock br. N. S. Chaffin preached from Acts 16, latter clause of the 30th verse : " What must I do to be saved."

At 11 o'clock br. M. May preached from Luke 16, latter part of the 8th verse : " For the children of this world are in their generation wiser than the children of light."

At 3 o'clock br. Albert Williams, from Georgia, preached from Heb. 7, 25 : " Wherefore he is able also to save them to the uttermost, that come unto God by him, seeing he ever liveth to make intercession for them."

The word preached had a powerful effect.

### MONDAY, AUGUST 16th, 1847.

Met according to adjournment. Prayer by br. Wm. Turner.

1. Called over delegates' names, and read the rules of decorum.

2. The Committee of Arrangements reported and were discharged.

3. The Committee of Finance reported that they had received from the churches $12 90 ; money paid over to the Treasurer ; and found in the Treasurer's hands $1 29, making in all $14 19. Committee discharged.

4. Corresponding messengers reported : Br. Wm. Turner, appointed to the Yadkin Association, attended, was cordially received, and had an interesting meeting ; the other brethren appointed, excused. Brn. J. Teague and A. Delap, attended Brier Creek, were cordially received, and had an interesting meeting ; br. Williams was excused. Br. A. Kinney attended the Pedee, and was cheerfully received. The brethren appointed to attend the Sandy Creek Association, failed to attend, and were excused. Br. William Turner, our delegate to the Convention, failed to attend, but forwarded the contributions by br. Robert J. Devin, who paid over the money to the Treasurer.

5. Appointed corresponding messengers to the following Associations : To the Yadkin, to be held the first Sunday in October, at Fork Church, brethren Wm. Turner, B. Lanier and J. Spurgen. To the Brier Creek, at Swan Creek meeting-house, on Saturday before the 4th Sabbath in September, brethren B. Lanier, A. Williams, Wm. Turner and A. Palmer. To the Pedee, to be held on Friday before the 4th Sabbath in October, at the ✕ Roads, brethren A. Kinney, E. H. Davis and Eli Coggen. To the Sandy Creek, to be held on Friday before the 4th Sabbath in September, brethren John Charles, Robert Goaly and Isaac A. Parks.

6. On motion, taken up correspondence with the Bulah Association again, to be held the first Sabbath in August, 1848; and we appoint brethren Wm. Turner, B. Lanier and Jonathan Merrell, to attend the same.

7. The Circular Letter, which was prepared by br. A Williams, was read and ordered to be attached to the minutes.

8. Appointed br. Wm. Turner to write the next circular letter.

9. The Committee on Church Letters and State of Religion reported, (see page 4) and was discharged.

10. The Committee on Sabbath Schools have nothing interesting to report : Committee discharged.

11. The Committee appointed to attend Jamestown Church, all failed to attend, except br. J. Spurgen, who reports that he finds them in an unfavorable condition. We recommend them not to dissolve, but continue; and we tender them our sympathies and prayer.

12. On motion, *Resolved*, That br. J. J. James have the privilege of publishing in the Recorder, the proceedings of this meeting, with their contributions for missions.

13. The collection taken up for Home Missions amounted to $12 85, and for foreign $7 66, making in all $20 52 ; and we appoint brethren Wm. Turner and E. H. Davis delegates, (B. Lanier in case of failure) to the Baptist State Convention, to bear the same.

14. The Association appoint the Clerk to write a letter requesting the Convention to aid them in employing a missionary among them.

15. The committee on the memorial have laid it on the table.

16. Appointed the next Association to be held at Reed's Roads, 5 miles West of Lexington, Davidson County, to commence on the Saturday before the 3d Lord's-Day in August, 1848.

17. Appointed br. B. Lanier to preach the introductory sermon; br. A. Williams his alternate.

18. *Resolved*, That this Association appoint brethren Azariah Williams, William Turner and Benjamin Lanier, Missionaries to labor two months each within the bounds of this Association, between this and next annual meeting; and we agree to pay them for their labors the sum of $20 each, per month.

19. *Resolved*, That this Association approve of the organization of a Southern Baptist Publication Society, the object of which is to promote among the Baptists a religious literature. *Resolved* also, that this body recommend to the churches the " Southern Journal," published in the city of Richmond, Virginia.

20. *Resolved,* That the thanks of this body be recorded in the minutes to the brethren and friends for their hospitality in supporting this meeting; and may the blessing of the Lord rest upon them.

21. We appoint the Clerk to attend to the printing of these minutes, (500 in number.)

22. After singing and prayer by Elder J. J. James, this body adjourned.

BENJAMIN LANIER, Moderator.

AZARIAH WILLIAMS, *Clerk.*

# REPORT
## on the State of Religion and Church Letters.

Your Committee on the State of Religion and Church Letters, beg leave to report: We have, with watchful eyes been endeavoring to observe the signs of the times; and we are sorry to say, that within the bounds of our Association, we have nothing interesting to report. When we look over the statistics of the Churches, we observe a great destitution of ministerial labor. We see that some of the churches are not supplied with preaching; and we cannot expect fruit, where there has been no labor bestowed. But the churches that have regular preaching, are in rather a cold state. Why is all this? Your committee is of the opinion that it is a subject which deserves your most serious attention. We sincerely hope that some plan will be speedily recommended, that the destitute churches may be supplied with regular preaching; and we would earnestly urge the necessity of searching to know the reason why the churches that are supplied with preaching, are in such a cold state. We know that it is not that the Almighty is not willing to bestow; we think that it is because we do not comply with the requisition of the Gospel. We earnestly desire therefore, that church members awake to their duty; that our ministers, in future, devote more of their time in reading and studying the Scripture; and we have no doubt that, before such united efforts, under the smile and direction of heaven, the powers of darkness will give back, and the true light of the Gospel will shine forth. And it will not be long until the tone of our reports and church letters will be very cheering. All of which is respectfully submitted.

WM. TURNER, Chairman.

# CIRCULAR.

DEAR BRETHREN: Permit us, in the present address, to call your attention to the importance of becoming spiritually or heavenly minded. We regret that our present limits barely afford room to hint in what it consists of, and how it is to be obtained. It consists of the following ingredients: Firstly, a deadness to the world; secondly, an eye habitually fixed on heaven, like Abraham, who looked for a city which hath foundations, whose builder and maker is God;—like the rest of that holy family, who, unmindful of the country from whence they came out, desired a better country, that is a heavenly, and confessed that they were strangers and pilgrims on earth. (These two ingredients are coupled together in those emphatic words to the Colossians: "If ye then be risen with Christ, seek those things which are above, where Christ sitteth at the right hand of God. Set your affections on things above, not on things on the earth; for ye are dead, and your life is hid with Christ in God.) Thirdly, such a walk with God as Enoch maintained, consisting in an intimate communion with Him, and consciousness of living in His presence; and consisting also in a will moving in the same line with His will, and leading to all that holy and beneficent action (under the form of obedience) which God himself pursues.

The heavenly mind thus constituted, is supported by that faith which is the substance of things hoped for, the evidence of things not seen. It is accompanied, of course, with an open view of God and Christ, and is conscious of God's universal agency, and depends on him for all things. It is familiar with his mercy and truth, and trusts him unwaveringly. It sees the reality and sincerity of the appointment of Christ to his mediatorial work, and is accustomed to contemplate his fitness and sufficiency for that work, his fullness and glory, and receives him as a complete and universal Saviour, with the full assurance of hope, which brings with it that peace of God which passeth all understanding. This is the heavenly mind. To attain this is the greatest happiness on this side of heaven. The man who possesses it lives in a world independent of the world without. Riches and friends, and even health may depart, but in this new world he finds a supply of all things. Amidst all the changes of life, he has here a stable inheritance. To possess this is far more than wealth or honor. It is the highest wisdom to bend all our attention to the acquisition of this. How then shall it be obtained? This is a question of the greatest personal importance to us. How can the heavenly mind be obtained?

My first remark is, that it must be received from God. Nor must we look for the gift from God, but through a mediator. But we must also realize that the blessing cannot come from God, but as the reward of Christ's righteousness; nor be dispensed with by any other hand than that of the mediatorial King. Nor must we overlook the personality and agency of the Holy Spirit. We must be sensible that this is the divine person who immediately does the whole work, and that the influence comes from Christ only as the spirit, in the economy of redemption, is placed under him as his reward. And because the whole furniture of a heavenly mind comes from God, my second direction is that we must ask him for it in a course of habitual and earnest prayer. The man who would rise up above the standing of ordinary christians, and attain to a heavenly mind, must be much in prayer. It cannot be gained by any other means. Not an instance can be found of one raised to this enviable height, who was not preeminently a man of prayer. The heavenly mind depends upon prayer. God could indeed give without prayer; and the indolent are ready to imagine that being unchangeable, he will bestow according to his eternal decree, whether men pray or not. But the truth is, that God acts according to the known laws of a holy mind, and bestows his richer favors only where there is an object to draw forth his special regard. Such an object is a praying saint. Thirdly, he must be much employed in heavenly meditation. The very idea of a heavenly mind is that it is familiar with heavenly things, and deeply affected by them. You cannot be familiar with a friend without frequent intercourse with him; you cannot be familiar with any art or practice, without repeated practice, so you cannot be familiar with heaven without frequently visiting it in your thoughts. Fourthly, the man who would attain to a heavenly mind, must be conscientious and punctual in his attendance on all the means of grace. It must not be a little thing that shall keep him from the House of God, or from prayer meeting. He must be systematic and inflexible in his private devotions, and in reading some portion of scripture every day. Fifthly, he must watch. This is a point of the utmost importance, and is frequently, in scripture, joined with prayer. Our hearts are a tinder box, ready to take fire from every spark; and the whole atmosphere around us being filled with scintillations as from a furnace, without the most constant watchfulness, some flame will secretly kindle which will burn up the whole frame of a heavenly mind. Watch the approaches of the enemy and all occasions of temptation. Watch your words and actions. Watch the approaches of Christ, and the motions of the Spirit. Watch for opportunities of doing good. The man who intends to live above the world and keep the face of heaven unclouded, must have his eyes about him. He must not suffer imaginations and thoughts and feelings to come and go as they please, without examination or care. A heavenly mind is a well regulated mind. In this, as much as in any thing, lies the difference between those eminent christians who walk with God, and those gay and easy professors who fall in with the manners of the world. One class are keeping their hearts with all diligence, and examining every object around them, and comparing it with the standard of the Word, and make this the daily toil and business of life. The other class flit along without examination or care; and if no actions or words escape them which the decent part of the world would condemn, they inquire no further. These are never likely to attain to a heavenly mind, and I am afraid they will never reach heaven itself. The man who would attain to the exalted dignity and serenity of a heavenly mind, must pursue a course of universal obedience. Every deliberate sin tends to grieve away the Spirit, and cut the sinews of faith and devotion, and prostrate the soul in the dust. I may further add, the man who would reach a heavenly mind, must be like God, much employed in doing good. The man of devotion without beneficence, may have some intercourse with his maker; and, in the ages of ignorance, when his neglect was winked at, might have had some elevated views of truth, but in these times of light, when the call for beneficent action is loudly heard from heaven and earth, he can never be admitted to an intimate walk with God. God will not walk with any man who is so unlike him; as with all their prayers, will not give a cent or put forth his hand to save a world from death.

It is necessary to the attainment of a heavenly mind, that a man possess a single eye—that he be not divided between the world and God, and keep a double object in view. To have two masters, or a double object, is to have an evil eye; to have a single object, as the one which controls the heart and life, is to have a single eye. None but those who answer the latter description, can live in the unclouded light of heaven. What saith the Scripture? If thine eye be single, thy whole shall be full of light; but if thine eye be evil [double] thy whole body shall be full of darkness. Those professors of religion, whose principal object, from month to month, is to get gain, will certainly never obtain a heavenly mind; and if there is any truth in the Bible, they will never reach heaven itself. Finally, a man cannot expect to ascend to this holy and happy elevation, without setting his mind upon it as the personal good to which all others must submit. He must determine to have this, whatever else is given up—to have it at all hazards and sacrifices,—to make every thing else bend and give way to this. He must say, God helping me, I must and will have this. Let every thing else go.

The man who thus resolves and perseveres, in the manner already described, will obtain this most desirable good, for God has promised success: Seek and ye shall find. The soul of the diligent shall be made fat. Delight thyself in the Lord, and he shall give thee the desires of thy heart. How much more shall your heavenly father give the Holy Spirit to them that ask him.

Here then is a good within the reach of every man, who will feel right and do his duty. And it is worth more in the present life than thrones and kingdoms. And now the question is, will you drop every other concern and rise up to this pursuit? Not one of you is excluded from spending your life high under the arch of heaven, far above the world, in full view of the heavenly city, knowing that to be your eternal home, and sheltered there from all the cares and troubles of life. The means by which you can make the ascent, have been pointed out. And now the question is, will you come up to this high and holy life, or will you grovel still in the dust, sighing, suffering, dying? There is but one mind that can answer the question, and that mind is your own. What say you now, my brethren? Will you start from your slumbers, and take hold of the strength of God and mount, or will you lose it all, and linger still in the dust?—If the latter, complain not hereafter of the want of comfort. If the troubles of life find you sleeping in their own domains, accuse not God. Be it remembered then that you had an opportunity to escape from them all, and live above their reach. If dismal doubts find you and break your peace, remember that you have none to blame but yourselves; for you had the offer of an abode in the confines of the New Jerusalem, surrounded with light that would have chased every fear away.

My brethren, you are all eager for happiness. Now the way is pointed out in which you may obtain it—a short way, the only way. You have met with disappointments in the world. Some of you have been unfortunate,—others of you have lost near and dear friends. You find below only what breaks your heart. Now then let us escape from all these, and live above their reach. Let us go up and be happy. Blessed be God for these tidings to sooth the anguished mind. Blessed be God for the offer of rest before we die. Our habitation here is desolate; thanks to his name that he has offered us abode so near his seat. O my soul, praise the Lord, and that is within me, praise his holy name forever. Amen.

AZARIAH WILLIAMS.

# A Table of Contents.

| CHURCHES. | COUNTIES | POST OFFICES | BY WHOM SUPPLIED | DELEGATES' NAMES. | Baptized | Rec. by letter | Restored | Dismissed | Excluded | Deceased | Total Numb's | Contribut'n's | Church Met. |
|---|---|---|---|---|---|---|---|---|---|---|---|---|---|
| Lick Creek, | Davidson, | Jackson Hill, | A. Kinney | A. Kinney, Jas Adderton, M Redwine | 1 | | | 1 | 1 | 1 | 39 | 1 50 | 4S |
| Jersey, | do | Cotton Grove, | Wm. Turner | Wm Turner Jno Merrell, J Wiseman | | 1 | | 4 | | | 196 | 2 00 | 1S |
| Abbot's Creek, | do | Browntown, | B. Lanier | J Spurgen, J Welch, Jno Teague | 5 | | | 1 | | | 381 | 00 | 3S |
| Tom's Creek, | de | Mt. Lebanon, | B. Lanier | B Lanier, J Lanier, P Riley | | | | | | | 25 | 75 | 1S |
| Jamestown, | Gulford | Jamestown, | | | | | | | | | 6 | 10 | 4S |
| Liberty, | Davidson | Fair Grove, | B. Lanier | B May, H Fouts, D Canoy | 1 | | | | 1 | | 44 | 92½ | 2S |
| Holloways, | do | Cotton Grove, | A. Kinney | C Smith, A Palmer, F Beanblossom | 1 | | | | | | 67 | 50 | 2S |
| New Friendship | Stokes | Salem, | | Jno Charles, J Styers, A Delapp | | | | | | | 13 | 72½ | 2S |
| Big Creek, | Montgomery | Wind Hill, | S. P. Moton | E H Davis, E Coggen, Wm Crouder | | | | | | 1 | 25 | 75 | 3S |
| Pine M. House, | Davidson | Jersey Settlement, | | E Nunly, R Barnes | | | | 2 | | | 81 | 00 | 4S |
| Reed's X Roads, | do | Lexington, | A. Williams | G Tussey, A Yarbrough, I A Parks | | | | | 1 | 3 | 48 | 50 | 2S |
| Marion, | do | do | *R. Goaly, | R Wetherington, J Green, R Goaly | 2 | | | 2 | 1 | | 35 | 50 | 1S |
| | | | | Total. | 10 | 1 | | 9 | 3 | 12 | 543 | 12 90 | 4S |

This Association has within its bounds four Ordained Preachers, to wit: A. Kinney, of Lick Creek; B. Lanier, of Tom's Creek;
Wm. Turner, of the Jersey; and A. Williams, of Reed's X Roads. And four Licentiates: G. Tussey, of Reed's X Roads; John
R. Owen and Robert Goaly, of Marion; and Dempsey Parks, of Lick Creek.
* At present, but not called by the Church.

# MINUTES

## OF THE
## SIXTEENTH ANNIVERSARY
### OF THE
# LIBERTY ASSOCIATION,
#### HELD AT
### REED'S CROSS ROADS CHURCH,
#### DAVIDSON COUNTY, N. C.,
#### (Five miles West of Lexington,)
*August the 19th and 21st days*, 1848.

---

1. The introductory discourse was delivered by Elder B. LANIER, from Isaiah 54 : 13. "All thy children shall be taught of the Lord, and great shall be the peace of thy children."

2. The Association was then organized by br. B. Lanier acting as Moderator *pro. tem.*

3. After singing and prayer by br. B. Lanier, letters from the churches were called for and read, and their contents noted. (See last page ) The Association then proceeded to elect br. B. LANIER *Moderator* for the term.

4. Opened the way for the reception of corresponding messengers: J. Oaks, from the Bulah Association, with minutes ; Eli Parker and S. S. Stone, from Pedee, with minutes ; R. Jacks, from Brier Creek, with minutes ; A. Roby, with minutes from the Yadkin Association.

5. Visiting brethren present were invited to seats, and to participate in our deliberations : the invitation was accepted by W. J. Witherington.

6. Appointed J. Spurgen, A. Kinney, J. Charles, P. Riley and J. W. Wiseman, with the Moderator and Clerk, a Committee of Arrangements.

7. Appointed brn. John Teague and D. L. Roach, a Committee of Finance.

8. Called for Circular prepared by br. Wm. Turner : presented, and referred to the Committee of Arrangements.

9. On motion, appointed br. Wm Turner, J. W. Wiseman and John Teague, a Committee on Church Letters and State of Religion, and gave them until Monday to report.

10. Called on the Committee on Sabbath Schools : On motion, gave them until Monday to report.

11. Appointed by ballot, br. R. Jacks, A. Roby and B. Lanier to occupy the stand on the Sabbath. Preaching to commence at 10 o'clock A. M.

12. On motion, agreed to adjourn until Monday, 9 o'clock. Prayer by br. R. Jacks.

---

## SABBATH.

The brethren appointed to occupy the stand, met a large and attentive congregation. Although it rained incessantly, they appeared inclined to hear the word preached.

Br. Benjamin Lanier occupied the stand at 10 o'clock, and preached from Heb. 2: 3. "How shall we escape, if we neglect so great salvation." Br. Richard Jacks, at 12 o'clock, from I Cor. 15: 58. "Therefore, my beloved brethren, be ye steadfast, unmovable, always abounding in the work of the Lord, for as much as ye know your labor is not in vain."

The word preached seemed to have a good effect.

From the inclemency of the weather, br. Roby had to decline preaching.

---

## MONDAY, AUGUST 21st.

1. Met according to adjournment; prayer by br. Richard Jacks.

2. Called over delegates' names, and read the rules of decorum.

3. The Committee of Arrangements reported and was discharged.

4. On motion, appointed one delegate from each church to examine the memorial presented by W. H. Hamner, consisting of James Adderton, J. W. Wiseman, John Teague, Peter Riley, N. Jarret, George Cross, John Charles, Eli Davis, Richard Barnes sen., A. R. Craver and Jesse Green.

5. Committee of Finance reported that they had received from the churches $12 75, and found in the hands of the Treasurer $1 19, making in all $13 94. Committee discharged.

6. Called on corresponding messengers to report: Wm, Turner reported that himself and br. Spurgen attended the Yadkin Association, and were cordially received. Br. B. Lanier gave satisfactory excuse. Br. A. Palmer attended the Brier Creek, and was cordially received; the other brethren who failed were excused. Br. Eli Coggen and the other brethren attended the Pedee, and were cordially received. The delegates appointed to the Sandy Creek were excused for not attending, not knowing the time and place. The brethren appointed to attend the Buhla, failed to attend, but wrote a letter to that body, which was received, and the brethren.

excused. Br. Wm. Turner, our delegate to the Convention, reported that he attended, paid over the money, was cordially received, and had an excellent meeting.

7. Appointed corresponding messengers to the following Associations: To the Yadkin, to be held at Bear Creek, on the first Sunday in October; brn. Wm. Turner, A. R. Craver and D. L. Roach. To Brier Creek, L. Terry, A. Delap, J. Spurgen and A. Kinney. To the Pedee, brn. Wm. Coggen, B. Lanier, M. Redwine and A. Williams; to be held on the 4th Sabbath in September. To Sandy Creek, brn. R. Witherington, R. Goaly and John Charles. To the Bulah, brn. L. Terry, Wm. Turner, A. Williams and J. W. Wiseman.

8. The Circular, which was prepared by br. Wm. Turner, was received and ordered to be printed and attached to the minutes.

9. Committee on Church Letters and on Religion, reported (see letter A) and was discharged.

10. The Committee on Sabbath Schools reported, (see letter B) and was discharged.

11. The brethren appointed to ride as missionaries, two months each, reported: Br. B. Lanier reported that he had attended several of the churches and received fifty cents compensation, and from various other causes could not ride the balance of the time. Br. A. Williams reported that he had spent some six days, received fifty cents, and from various other causes, could not attend the balance of the time. Br. Wm. Turner reported that he had labored 16 days, preached 16 sermons, traveled 226 miles, received $2 88¼ cents. The balance was paid by the Association.

12. The collection taken up for Home Missions, amounted to $10 05; and we appoint br. Wm. Turner our delegate to the Baptist State Convention, to bear the same.

13. We appoint the next Association to be held at Big Creek Church, Montgomery County, to commence on Saturday before the 3d Sabbath in August, 1849.

14. Appointed br. A. Williams to preach the introductory sermon; br. Wm. Turner his alternate.

15. We appoint br. Richard Jacks to ride six months within its bounds, during the Associational year; and we agree to pay him $25 00 per month for his services.

16. The committee appointed to examine the memorial of Wm. H. Hamner, report that they think it not expedient to bring up the same before the Association; therefore it is laid by.                                    JOHN CHARLES, Chairman.

17. *Resolved*, That the thanks of this body be recorded in the minutes to the brethren and friends for their hospitality in supporting this meeting; and may the blessing of the Lord rest upon them.

18. We appoint the Clerk to attend to the printing of the minutes, 500 in number.)

19. After singing and prayer by br. Wm. Turner, adjourned.

BENJAMIN LANIER, *Moderator.*

AZARIAH WILLIAMS, *Clerk.*

---

## A.

Your Committee on the State of Religion and Church Letters regret that they have to say, that several of the letters represent the churches in a lukewarm condition; having had but little or no refreshing during the Associational year. From observation, however, your committee think that there is a growing interest for the cause of the Redeemer, within our bounds. Some of the Churches have had some accessions during the past year; and throughout the length and breadth of the Association, there is an unusual anxiety manifested for ministerial labor.

We do think that the present state of things amongst us, calls loudly for each one to be up and doing. The day of our salvation is at hand: soon the night will come, when no man can work.

We do hope that *some plan* will be speedily adopted, so that, to the poor and destitute, the gospel may be preached. All of which is respectfully submitted.

WM. TURNER, *Chairman.*

## B.

### REPORT ON SABBATH SCHOOLS.

The Committee have nothing of importance to relate on the above named subject. Our churches generally speak favorably to Sabbath Schools, but do very little towards encouraging them in any way whatever. There appears from the reading of the letters sent up to the Association, from the different churches composing the same, to be no Sabbath Schools in successful operation amongst them. Dear brethren, we are far behind many of our sister Associations upon this subject, which we consider of great importance. Therefore we hope the delegates composing this Association will try to stir up the churches to which they belong, upon this subject; and if possible, get up Sabbath Schools and have them in successful operation as soon as possible. For we believe these are good nurseries for the training of the minds of the youth of our beloved country. May we, in all we think or do, have reference to the glory of God, and the good of immortal souls. Respectfully submitted.

BENJAMIN LANIER, *Chairman.*

# Circular.

DEAR BRETHREN:

ANGER is the subject of the present address. All the disorder which reigns within us, and the follies which constantly appear in our outward demeanor, arise from an abuse of our faculties through ages, as the streams which issue from a corrupted fountain. To this general source we may trace violent anger. But, to be a little more particular, we will mention some of the causes of anger.

1. Pride.—A contentious spirit, inspiration assures us, originates in pride. *Only by pride cometh contention.* It is pride that makes men passionate. They cannot bear the least slight, or that which hath the appearance of it, because they think themselves of so much importance. We have a remarkable instance of this in Haman: He is enraged, filled with indignation, and breathes nothing but revenge. The life of an individual cannot suffice; the blood of a whole nation must be shed to cool his wrath and lay his vengeance to sleep. What is the cause of this desolating decree? An individual fails to pay him that idolatrous obeisance of which he thought himself so worthy. Who does not see that if it should be asked, *What meaneth the heat of this great anger?* the answer must be it originates in pride. It is pride that fills the world with so much animosity. We forget what we are, in the fullness of self esteem.

2. Ignorance is more frequently the cause of sinful anger.—A weak mind is easily kindled into resentment. A wise man may be angry, when there is a sufficient cause for it, but his anger is restrained by prudence and discretion.

3. Not duly watching over our own spirits.—The word of command given us by the Captain of our salvation is, *Take heed to your spirit.* Mal 2 : 15. They that would be kept from sin, must keep a jealous eye upon their hearts; for there all sin begins. *Take heed to thyself, and keep thy soul diligently,* was the charge which God gave to his ancient people. (Deut. 4 : 9,) It is not enough to guard our eyes, our ears, our hands or feet; the heart itself should be carefully guarded and kept.

4. Not considering the evil of sinful anger.—A meek and quiet spirit is of such real value, that God himself beholds it with delight, and puts a high value upon it: It is *in the sight of God of great price.* (I Pet. 3 : 4.) If an angry man gains any influence by his bluster and noise, he pays dear for his power. He forfeits his own tranquility, he loses the friendship of his equals, and incurs the hatred of his dependents.

5. Not duly considering the object which provokes us.—Nothing

can be a stronger proof of a man's weakness, than his suffering his fiery passions to rise and flame before he knows whether there be any occasion. We should never be angry at a child, a servant, or a friend, till we see, from a clear and impartial survey of circumstances, that we have just reasons to be so.

Though we are not absolutely forbidden to be angry, yet happy is he who has the least occasion for it. The divine rule is short, but very comprehensive: *Be angry and sin not.* Our present business is to consider when we transgress this divine law.

1. When we are angry with the providence of God, our anger is sinful. The events of Providence are sometimes grievous and afflictive; they cross our inclinations, and seem to oppose our secular interests. Yet it becomes us not to be angry, sullen and impatient.—We have not, I think, a more striking instance of the power of anger against the conduct of Divine Providence, than what appears in the character of Jonah. That angry prophet was displeased with the forbearance and long-suffering of the Almighty: so much so, that he wished himself to die, and said, *It is better for me to die than to live.* The God of patience asked him, *Dost thou well to be angry?* And he said, *I do well to be angry even unto death!* Strange! to be angry at God, and angry too for a gourd: and still to justify his passion in the face of his Maker! How unaccountably anger blinds the mind, that a man under the influence of it should make light of sin, and bid defiance to death: nay, should even in the presence of the divine Creator, justify his rage, and wish to die under the influence of so bad, so shocking a disposition!—

2. When we are angry at the good we see in others.—Thus Joseph was hated for his dreams, and for his words; and Daniel for his continuance in prayer and supplication to his God. Cain, the wicked one, slew his brother, *because his own works were evil, and his brother's righteous.* Perhaps there is no species of anger so diabolical as this—to be angry with others because of their excellencies.

3. When we are angry with those who differ from us in religious sentiments.—Why should I be displeased with any man for his differing from me in his religious opinions? He has the same reason to be angry with me for the liberty I have thought proper to assume. The right of private judgment was asserted by our Lord Jesus Christ in the whole of his ministry. He charged his disciples to *call no man master on earth;* and exhorted the people to *search the Scriptures,* and so to judge for themselves. The apostle Paul and his fellow apostles, maintained this right. *Let every man be fully persuaded in his own mind.* Their hearers assumed this privilege, and *searched the Scriptures daily whether these things were so.* What pity it is that mankind should ever have pursued an opposite course; and that christianity should ever have been so explained, as to promote all the violent and resentful passions of which human nature, in its deepest

depravity, is capable, and to patronize the bloodiest cruelties that the world ever beheld! Surely there can be nothing so directly opposite, as religion and revenge, piety and persecution, prayer and plunder, the service of God, and the slaughter or oppressing of those who bear his image. Heat and violence, anger and resentment in religious disputes, naturally lead on to persecution. *Let all bitterness, and wrath, and clamor, and evil-speaking, be put away from you, with all malice. And be ye kind one to another, tender-hearted, forgiving one another, even as God, for Christ's sake, hath forgiven you.*

4. When we are angry at reproof.—The wrathful man flies in the face of his reprover, and says with the Egyptian to Moses, *Who made thee a Judge over us?* (Exod. 2 : 14.) It is most ungrateful to be angry with a kind reprover, who has our welfare at heart, and warns us of that which would be pernicious to us; then, if ever, our anger is to be condemned. When he that reproveth in the gate, is hated for his faithfulness, it may truly be said that iniquity abounds, and love waxeth cold. If we do that which deserves a rebuke, and our friends are so just and kind as to deal faithfully with us, we ought not to quarrel with them, and return hatred for their love : we should suffer the word of exhortation, and take it patiently and kindly. The reprover may magnify the offence ; his admonition may be defective in point of prudence ; yet in the main, it is a real instance of kindness, and it would be highly criminal to resent it. *As an ear-ring of gold, and an ornament of fine gold, so is a wise reprover upon an obedient ear.*

In conclusion, though it may not be within our power to prevent anger, yet it is our privilege and duty to suppress it, and keep it within proper bounds. Therefore, when we feel our temper ruffled, let us be silent, and cherish it not, and a calm will ensue. The divine command is, *Let not the sun go down upon your wrath.* Withall, let us observe the broad command of our Saviour, *I say unto all, Watch.* May the God of peace help us so to do. AMEN.

**WM. TURNER.**

# A Table of Contents.

| CHURCHES. | COUNTIES. | POST OFFICES. | BY WHOM SUPPLID | DELEGATES' NAMES. | Baptized | Rec by Letter | Restored | Dis. by Letter | Excluded | Deceased | Whites | Colored | Total Number | Funds | Ch. Meetings |
|---|---|---|---|---|---|---|---|---|---|---|---|---|---|---|---|
| Lick Creek | Davidson | Jackson Hill | A Kinney | A Kinney, James Adderton, M Rodwin | 1 | | | 3 | | | 34 | 1 | 36 | 1 50 | 48 |
| Jersey | do | Cotton Grove | Wm. Turner | Wm Turner, D L Roach, J W Wiseman | 79 | | | 2 | | 6 | 136 | 135 | 271 | 2 62 | 18 |
| Abbott's Creek | do | Abbotts creek | B Lanier | Joseph Spurgen, John Tengue, R. Crouch | 5 | | | | | | 43 | | 43 | 1 00 | 18 |
| Tom's Creek | do | Mt. Lebanon | B Lanier | B Lanier, J Lanier, Peter Riley | | | | | | | 23 | 2 | 25 | 1 00 | 18 |
| Jamestown | do | Jamestown | B. Lanier | | | | | | | | | | | | |
| Liberty | do | Fair Grove | B. Lanier | J Fine, N Jarret, H Copple | | | | | | | 42 | 1 | 43 | 80 | 28 |
| Holloways | Davidson | Cotton Grove | A. Kinney | George Cross, J Cross, A Leanblossom | 11 | | | 9 | | | 52 | 26 | 78 | 1 15 | 28 |
| New Friendship | do | Salem | A. Kinney | J Charles, A Delap, L Terry | | 1 | | 1 | | | 16 | | 16 | 50 | 28 |
| Big Creek | Stokes | Wind Hill | S. P. Moton | Wm R Coggen, Eli Davis, Wm Hamelton | 12 | 3 | | 3 | | | 39 | 4 | 43 | 80 | 35 |
| Pine M. House | Montgomery | Lexington | Wm R Coggen | E Nunley, R Barnes, W Nunlev. R Barnes, jr. | 10 | 1 | | 1 | | | 18 | 1 | 19 | 1 00 | 35 |
| Reed's X Roads | Davidson | do | C. Bissent | A R Craver, B Myers, J Cornish | | | | | 2 | 1 | 44 | | 44 | 1 56 | |
| Marion | do | do | A. Williams | R Witherington, J Green, A Witherington | | | | | 3 | 2 | 26 | 2 | 28 | 87 | 43 |
| | | | | | 121 | 4 | 4 | 11 | 2 | 9 | 473 | 173 | 646 | 12 75 | |

This Association has within its bounds four Ordained Preachers, to wit: A. Kinney, of Lick Creek; B. Lanier, of Tom's Creek; Wm. Turner, of the Jersey; and A. Williams, of Reed's X Roads. And two Licentiates: G. Tussey, of Reed's X Roads; and Robert Goaly, of Marion.

# MINUTES

OF THE

## EIGHTEENTH ANNIVERSARY

OF THE

# LIBERTY ASSOCIATION,

HELD AT

JAMESTOWN CHURCH, GUILFORD CO., N. C.

August the 16th, 17th, and 19th, 1850.

Salisbury:

PRINTED AT THE CAROLINA WATCHMAN OFFICE.

1850.

# MINUTES.

—

1. The Introductory Sermon was delivered by brother B. LANIER, from 1 Cor., 13, last verse.

2. The Association was organized by brother B. Lanier acting as Moderator.

3. After singing and prayer by brother B. Lanier, letters from the Churches were handed in, read, and their contents noted. (See last page.) The Association then proceeded by ballot to elect brother B. LANIER Moderator for the present Term.

4. On motion, appointed a Committee to examine the letter and brethren from Salisbury Church, the Committee to consist of one Delegate from each Church with Ministering brethren. Brother M. Redwine, William Turner, Jno. Teague, Jno. Robeson, Joel Moody, B. May, A. Palmer, Alex. Delap, Eli Coggin, A. Williams, R. Witherington,—the Committee to report on Saturday morning.

5. Opened the way for the reception of corresponding brethren.— Brethren Jno. Robeson, Ja. Lanier, J. J. James, N. J. Palmer,, and, on motion, received Julius Terrell, all from the Bulah; N. S. Chaffin, C. W. Bessent, Uriah Huffman, from the Yadkin; from the Sandy Creek, E. Crutchfield, S. Barker, E. Elliott.

6. Visiting brethren present invited to take a seat with us. A. M. Rockwell accepted the invitation.

7. Appointed brethren Wm. Turner, Jo. Spurgen, A. Palmer, B. May, R. Witherington, with the Clerk and Moderator, a Committee of Arrangements.

8. Appointed brethren Ja. Wiseman, Jno. Teague, a Committee of Finance.

9. Appointed brethren Wm. Turner, Z. Minor, John Charles, a Committee on Church letters and state of Religion.

10. On motion by J. Spurgen, appointed a Committee consisting of the Delegates of Jamestown Church, with brethren J. Welch and J.

Spurgen, to arrange preaching during the Association with the exception of the Sabbath.

11. Called for Circular letters, and, on motion, referred to the Committee of Arrangements.

12. Appointed brethren Wm. Turner, Jno. Teague, a Committee, and John Willson, J. Robeson, to examine into the expediency of a Bible Society, and Education, &c.

13. On motion, agreed to adjourn until 10 o'clock, A. M. Prayer by J. Robeson.

---

SATURDAY, AUGUST 17.

Met according to adjournment. Prayer by brother Wm. Turner.

1. On motion, the Report of the Committee of Arrangements. Received.

2. On motion, agreed to have the Articles of Faith attached to the Minutes.

3. The Committee appointed to examine the Constitution of the Salisbury Church, reported and was dismissed.

4. On motion, read the petition from the Salisbury Church, with their Faith and Church Covenant; and being found orthodox, was received into this body.

5. Committee of Finance reported that they had received from the

| | | |
|---|---|---|
| Churches | $16 | 04 |
| Remaining in Clerk's hands | | 11 |
| | $16 | 15 |

Committee discharged.

6. The Committee on Publications, Sabbath Schools, Bible Society, &c., reported that it is necessary to have Committees appointed. Committee discharged.

On motion of brother Rockwell, appointed brethren Jno. Robeson, Jno. Teague, A. Palmer, a Committee on Sabbath Schools and Publication Society.

Brethren Wm. Turner, A. Williams, B. May, on Domestic Missions.

A. M. Rockwell, Wm. Lambeth, Jno. A. Weirman, on Bible Society, and report on Monday.

On motion, called until 2 o'clock.

After singing and prayer by J. J. James, the Association resumed business.

7. Correspondents to sister Associations were called on to report, which was done as far as present, and gave encouraging accounts; those that failed were excused.

8. On motion, the Association then proceeded to appoint correspondents to sister Associations, when the following appointments were made: To the Yadkin, to commence the Saturday before the first Sunday in October at New Hope in Iredell, B. Lanier, A. Williams, Aaron Yarbrough. To Brier Creek, brethren Wm. Turner, Z. Minor, Wm. Lambeth, to be held on the 4th Sabbath in September, at Zion Meetinghouse, Iredell County. To Sandy Creek, to commence on Friday before the 1st Sabbath in October at Moon's Chapel, brethren Wm. Turner, J. Moody, Jno. Charles, James Greenwood. To the Pedee, in Stanly County, Ebenezer Church, on Friday before the fourth Sunday in September, brethren A. Kinney, B. Lanier, Eli Coggin. To the Bulah, to commence on Friday before the third Sabbath in August, 1851, in Forsythe, at Goodwill Church, brethren Wm. Turner, Jno. Teague, B. Lanier, A. Williams, D. Raper. To the Jefferson Association, being so far and coming so near each other, on motion, agreed to drop correspondence on friendly terms.

9. On motion, proceeded to elect by ballot brethren J. J. James, Jno. Robeson, E. Crutchfield, to occupy the Stand on the Sabbath, and preach a Missionary sermon at 11 o'clock.

10. On motion, adjourned until Monday 9 o'clock. Prayer by E. Crutchfield.

## SABBATH.

The brethren appointed to occupy the Stand, met a large and attentive congregation.

Elder Enoch Crutchfield, from Sandy Creek, occupied the Stand at 10 o'clock, and preached from I Cor. 7 and latter clause of the 31st verse. Elder J. J. James, Agent of the Convention, from I Tim. 3, 15 v. at 11 o'clock, and brother Jno. Robeson, at 3 o'clock, from Heb. 9, 27—28 v. The congregation was attentive, the word preached seemed blessed to the edifying of christians and conviction of sinners.

MONDAY, AUGUST 19, 1850.

1. Met according to adjournment. Prayer by Elder Robeson.

Called for the Circular; read, and ordered to be attached to the Minutes.

2. On motion, agreed to have no Circular next year.

3. On motion, called on the Missionary to report. See letter A, reported and received.

4. On motion, called on Committee of state of Religion and Church letters, to report. Reported and dismissed. See letter B.

5. The Committee on Domestic Missions reported and dismissed. See letter C.

6. On motion of J. J. James, agreed to alter the time of holding the Association until Friday before the fourth Sabbath in August, and the next Session is to be held with the Liberty Church, Davidson, N. C.

7. Appointed brother Wm. Turner to preach the Introductory Sermon; brother A. Williams, his alternate.

8. N. J. Palmer appeared on Monday, as correspondent of Bulah, and, on motion, was received by the Moderator giving the hand of fellowship.

9. On motion by brother Robeson, agreed to have a Missionary the next year, and proceeded to elect brother N. Heriford our Missionary next year.

Called for one hour.

10. Took up business again.

11. On motion of brother Robeson, the resolution of last year concerning Licentiates is rescinded, and farther we appoint the Ordained Ministers of this Association, and Pastors of the Churches within the Association, to be a Standing Presbyter, and three of them to form a quorum, to ordain Ministers and Deacons, and constitute Churches.

12. On motion of brother N. J. Palmer, the following resolution was unanimously adopted by the Association: -

WHEREAS, in the opinion of this Association, it is of the utmost importance that Literary Schools, both male and female, under the patronage of the Baptist denomination, or the management of able and competent members of our Church, should be liberally sustained, therefore,

*Resolved*, That this Association commend to the support of their brethren and friends throughout its bounds, Wake Forest College—the Cherry Hill Male Institute (near Milton,) under the management of Elder John H. Lacy—the Male Academy in Rockingham County, under the management of brother S. Ivey—the Milton Female Seminary under the management of Rev. Archibald McDowell and Lady, at Milton, N.

C., and the Rockford Female Institute under the management of Rev. E. W. West and Lady, as schools eminently worthy of their confidence and patronage.

On motion of brother J. J. James, the following resolution was also unanimously adopted by the Association:

WHEREAS, the establishment of a Female Institution of high character, to be under the control of the Baptist denomination in this State, has been for some time exciting attention, therefore,

*Resolved*, That this Association is fully persuaded of the necessity and importance of establishing such an Institution and will be ready to co-operate in the measure.

The Committee on the Bible, Sunday School and Publication Society, reported. (See letter D.) Committee discharged.

13. *Resolved*, That we have a Board of Managers, consisting of the Ordained Ministers of this Association and a member from each Church, and that each Church appoint a member at their next monthly meeting, and that the Board have the power of contracting with the Missionary and direct him where to perform his labors.

14. Whereas it appears that we have no Book in general use, and feeling the necessity of having a standard Book adopted among us, therefore,

*Resolved*, That we recommend to the Churches composing this Association that they adopt the Psalmist as their standard Book.

*Resolved*, That we recommend to the Churches composing this Association to observe the Friday before the 4th Lord's day in October as a day of Fasting and prayer to Almighty God, for a revival of religion in the bounds of this Association, and throughout the world.

On motion of N. J. Palmer, we appoint B. Lanier, A. Williams, Delegates to represent us in the next Baptist State Convention to be held at Louisburg, Franklin County.

On motion,

*Resolved*, That the sincere thanks of this Association be tendered to the brethren and friends for their kindness in supporting this meeting during its session.

After singing and prayer by brother N. J. Palmer, this Association adjourned to the time and place.

B. LANIER, Moderator.

AZARIAH WILLIAMS, Clerk.

# CIRCULAR.

Dear Brethren, composing the Liberty Association: The time has arrived when we have to appear before you in the form of a Circular; and we know of no better subject upon which to address you than that of *Charity*. It appears to be a principle that our Savior admonished his disciples to cultivate, and is highly appreciated throughout the Sacred Writings.

The Apostle Paul, after naming several other graces, tells us that, without Charity, we are nothing.

A charitable spirit is not a mere disposition to give alms to the poor; this is only one of its many good effects; it is rather that mind that was in Christ Jesus; which prompted him to love mankind in their sins, and to determine him to save them at the expense of his own precious blood. And we are admonished to let more of that mind be in us that was in Christ.

By one writer, Charity is defined to be a principle of love to God and good will to men; wishing well to all. A charitable spirit in a christian is the fountain from which most of the other graces spring— whence all the good, practiced among men, takes its origin.

Forbearance, forgiveness, long-suffering under injuries, gentleness, mildness, &c., are some of its many fruits. Feeding the hungry, clothing the naked, visiting the sick, acting the part of a father to the fatherless, of a friend to the friendless, to make another's sufferings our own, to rejoice with those that rejoice and to weep with those that weep, are a part of its holy works. It abhors the appearance of sin under any color; being possessed of a true spirit of love, we view the faults of our brethren with heart-felt sorrow, and those of our enemies with forbearance and forgiveness. It is a spirit that never aggravates nor propagates the follies of others: it spreads its mantle over a multitude of faults, and would fain blot them out of existence.

Envy, evil speaking, back-biting, pride, and selfishness, flee from her train; faithfulness, candor, prudence, philanthropy, and happiness, are its constant attendants. It sometimes wounds, yet never but with a view to healing. If it frowns, it is the frown of reform; and its chastisements are the chastisements of peace. In prosperity, it warns not to be too much elated, and in adversity, it strengthens the feeble knees, and lifts up the hands which hang down. It is heaven-born, and nurtured near the Eternal Throne; and it renders our condition easy in any circumstances in life. It is a visitant on earth, going about pointing out the road to glory and happiness, and leading all to the abodes of peace, who will follow its advice and example. It is a plant of Paradise, which never thrives in human soil, unless moistened with the dew of heaven, and cultivated according to the rules laid down in the New Testament. It seeks no rank on earth, but with equal readinss becomes a guest to the prince or the peasant, the sovereign or his subjects. Faith and hope are its principal ministers in this world. So we conclude, that it is placed within the reach of all the children of men, who desire it; and Solomon in his Proverbs, tells us that the desire accomplished, is sweet to the soul.

Are we, brethren, possessed of a true spirit of Charity?—that kind that seeks not her own, but the welfare of all mankind? In the out-set, we said that it was a principle of love to God, and benevolence to men; which inclines the possessor to glorify God, and to do good to others. Its distinguishing characteristics may be seen in I Cor. 13, which the Apostle concludes by saying, "And now abideth faith, hope, charity, these three, but the greatest of these is charity." And now, brethren, it remains for us to prove what graces we possess by the works that they produce in us; for it seems that the Apostle James would inquire after graces without their corresponding works. Now, in order that we be useful members in society, and grow in grace, we should open our sinful and contracted hearts, to the influence of the Holy Spirit, and, as the Apostle would have it, let God work in us both to will and to do of his own good pleasure. When we look around us, and see the destitution of some of our Churches, remembering at the same time, that we have Ministers enough to supply them with regular preaching, an inquiry arises, where are they? We might answer, that they are attending to their temporal matters, instead of administering to the spiritual necessities of the Churches, and breaking the bread of life from house to house, as was the practice in the Apostolic age, because the Churches have neglected to administer to their temporal wants. Dear brethren, these things ought not so to be. Is there not bread enough and to spare, in the bounds of our Association, that the hands of our Ministers might be untied from their temporal concerns, and they set at liberty, to dispense the words of Eternal Life, throughout the length and breadth of our

Association; visiting from house to house, teaching those things that pertain to eternal life; thereby having access to hundreds that they could not otherwise? We well know, that though all success is from God, and that to him all glory is due, there is much for the Church to do in evangelizing the world. Though they go forth in tears, sowing precious seed, yet shall they return rejoicing, bringing their sheaves with them. And if we have administered to their temporal necessities, so as to liberate them, that they may sow those precious seeds in abundance, shall we not be partakers of their joys when the Great Head of the Church shall look down on our labors of love, and shall see the travail of his soul, and shall be satisfied? Let us come up to the help of the Lord against the mighty: put our shoulders to the Gospel wheel, relying on the precious promise, "Lo, I am with you always," and we shall soon see the desert blossom as the rose. May God, in his love wherewith He loved us, sanctify you through his truth, to his name's honor and glory. Amen.

----

### A.
### MISSIONARY'S REPORT.

JAMESTOWN, GUILFORD COUNTY, AUGUST 17, 1850.

DEAR BRETHREN : Since my appointment as Missionary to the Liberty Association, I have travelled 2,134 miles; labored 6 months; received $3 12½; preached 137 sermons; attended 5 protracted meetings in the bounds of this Association. At Jamestown, there were 16 professed faith in the Redeemer. At Liberty, there were 28 hopefully converted to the Lord. At Tom's Creek 3.

All of which is respectfully submitted,

W. N. HERIFORD.

----

### B.
### REPORT ON STATE OF RELIGION AND CHURCH LETTERS.

Your Committee, on the state of Religion and Church Letters, beg leave to report: That there is a more interesting state of things amongst us than has been for many years; considerable revivals have taken place in different sections of the Association, within the past year. The Church letters give cheering evidence of the growing interest that is being taken in the cause of our blessed Redeemer. But there is great reason for renewed effort on our part; as there are sections, even within our own bounds, that are very destitute of Baptist preaching; and we should not consider our duty done, until the Gospel, and its benefits are enjoyed by the inhabitants of the earth.

All of which is respectfully submitted,

WM. TURNER, Ch'm'n.

---

### C.

Your Committee, to whom was referred the subject of Home Missions, have had the matter under consideration. They are of opinion that the Gospel influence in our Association is far too small, and that it is our duty, as an Associated body, to do all in our power to extend the Re·deemer's kingdom.

The purity of society, as well as, the happines of our own domestic hearths, needs more of the sacred influence of the Gospel in our bounds.

Isolated cases of personal piety may be found here and there throughout our Association, and we have many very worthy members among us; yet we feel to lament the great want of personal piety among our members. Is it not too much the case that the difference is not visible between the professor and non-professor? and that sometimes the member of the Church is disparaged by comparison with the non-professor?

If each Church would maintain a faithful Minister, so that his time and talents could be devoted to the spread of the Gospel, the call for a Missionary would not be so great.

We feel it the bounden duty of this Associated body, in its associated capacity, to provide, by its councils and its energy, for the faithful preaching of the words of eternal life. Our children and companions as well as our own eternal interests require that we should be faithful in this matter.

If our Pastors are so engaged in the temporal affairs of this world as to have little or no time to devote to the interests of our beloved Zion, let us look abroad for such help as we can get through a Missionary.

A. WILLIAMS, Ch'm'n.

---

### D.

Your Bible, Sunday School, and Publication Society, Committee feel it their duty to report in favor of, the adoption of the most efficient means of operation.

The Bible lies in our houses unread and unstudied by many.

How shall this evil be corrected? Your Committee think Sunday Schools the most reliable source—in fact, almost the only source.

A man that can read, can teach the Bible if the grace of God be in his heart. We want kind and affectionate teaching. Your Committee would recommend that this subject be laid before our Churches early next spring, both by the Pastors of the Churches and by the Missionary, and that Sunday Schools be organized in 'every neighborhood.

Your Committee most earnestly recommend the formation of a Society by this Association, that it may concentrate the efforts of the friends of Zion.

All of which is respectfully submitted,

JOHN ROBERTSON.

## LIBERTY BIBLE AND PUBLICATION SOCIETY.

Immediately after the adjournment of the Association, the members agreed to form a Bible and Publication Society, auxiliary to the North Carolina Baptist Publication and Sunday School Society.

Elder BENJAMIN LANIER, was called to the Chair, and brother N. J. Palmer, requested to act as Secretary, pro tem.

The following Constitutiou was then submitted for the adoption of the Society:

ARTICLE 1.—This Society shall be called THE LIBERTY BIBLE AND PUBLICATION SOCIETY, and shall be auxiliary to the North Carolina Baptist Publication and Sunday School Society.

ARTICLE 2.—The objects of the Society shall be the establishment of a Depository of Bibles and Religious Books, and Tracts, at some convenient point within the bounds of the Liberty Association, where our Sabbath Schools and Churches, and others, may be supplied with Bibles and Testaments, and suitable religious books for their use at cheap rates. Also, to give all proper encouragement to the establishment and support of Sabbath Schools in all our Churches and neighborhoods.

ARTICLE 3.—The Society shall hold its annual meetings with the Liberty Association, and some one shall be selected annually to deliver an Address or Sermon before the Society on the Saturday afternoon of the Association. Intermediate meetings of the Society may be called and held under the direction of the President or one of the Vice Presidents.

ARTICLE 4.—The Officers of the Society shall be a President, three Vice Presidents, Secretary, Treasurer and Depository Agent, who shall be annually chosen by the Society. Also a Board of Managers to attend to the business of the Society in the interval of its meetings.

ARTICLE 5.—Any one may become a member of the Society by contributing annually to its funds; or by the payment of Ten Dollars at any one time become a Life Member of the Society.

ARTICLE 6.—The Board of Managers shall have the disposition of the funds of the Society in the interval of its annual meetings, and appoint one or more Agents or Col-porteurs. Five members of the Board shall constitute a quorum to do business.

ART. 7.—The Board of Managers and the Treasurer and Depository Agent must make an annual Report of their operations to the Society.

The above Constitution having been read, was unanimously adopted by the Society.

The following Officers were then elected for the ensuing year:

Elder WILLIAM TURNER, *President.* JAMES WISEMAN, ALEXANDER DELAP, and JOHN TEAGUE, *Vice Presidents.*

JOHN A. WEIRMAN, of Salisbury, *Secretary,* and ROBERT GOALY, of Lexington, N. C., *Treasurer* and *Depository Agent.*

## BOARD OF MANAGERS.

The Officers of the Society, with Elder Benjamin Lanier, Chairman, Elder Azariah Williams, Richard Witherington, Henry Copple, James Greenwood, Davis Raper, Jesse Styres, Aaron Yarbrough, Dr. James W. Wiseman, Daniel L. Roach. W. N. Heriford, and John Redwine.

On motion, Elder J. B. Solomon was appointed to deliver the next annual Sermon or Address before the Society.

The Churches within the bounds of the Liberty Association are requested to hold one or more meetings at their several Meeting-houses during the ensuing year, and to raise funds and send them up to the Treasurer by the Missionary of the Association or other safe opportunity. Also to establish Sabbath Schools in each Church.

The Officers of this Society, together with the Delegates of the Association to the Baptist State Convention, are requested to represent this Society at the annual meeting of the State Society at Louisburg, N. C., in October next.

On motion, it was ordered, that the proceedings of this meeting with the Constitution of the Society, be published with the Minutes of the Association at the expense of the Society.

On motion, the Society then adjourned.

BENJAMIN LANIER, *Chairman.*

N. J. PALMER, *Secretary, pro tem.*

N. B.—All orders for Books, or remittances of funds, to be made to Robert Goaly, Treasurer and Depository Agent, Lexington, N. C.

---

Your Committee beg leave to report the following

## ARTICLES OF FAITH.

We believe that the Holy Bible was written by men divinely inspired; that it is a perfect rule of faith and practice; and that among others it teaches the following truths:

1. That there is one living and true God: eternal, immortal, invisible and only wise; and that he has revealed himself as the Father, and the Son, and the Holy Ghost; the same in essence, and equal in divine qualities. I Tim. 1, 17; I John 5, 7.

2. That man was created in the image of God, in uprightness and true holiness: but by wilfully violating the law of his Maker, he fell from that state; so that by nature there is in us no holiness; for we are all inclined to evil; and in that all have sinned, all are children of wrath, justly exposed to death. Gen. 1, 27; Eph. 4, 24; Eph. 2, 3.

3. That salvation is by grace through faith in Christ, (and that not of yourselves, it is the gift of God;) who, miraculously assumed our nature, sin only excepted, for the suffering of death. Eph. 2, 8.

4. That nothing can separate true believers from the love of God: but that they will be kept by the power of God through faith unto salvation, the sure and final proof of their being true believers, consisting in their patient continuance in well-doing. Rom. 8, 38, 39; Rom. 2, 7.

5. That a Church is a congregation of baptized believers; whose only officers are Bishops or Pastors, and Deacons. And that there are but two Sacraments, Baptism, and the Lord's Supper.

6. That the proper subjects of the ordinance of Baptism are true believers; and that Baptism is Immersion. Acts 8, 37; Rom. 6, 4.

7. That the Sacrament of the Lord's Supper is to be observed *in the Church* till the second coming of Christ. I Cor. 11, 26.

8. That there will be a resurrection of the just and unjust; and that the Lord Jesus Christ will come to judge the quick and dead; and then the wicked will go away into everlasting punishment, and the righteous into life eternal. Acts 24, 15; I Thess. 4, 16; Matt. 25, 46.

# TABLE OF CONTENTS.

| CHURCHES. | COUNTIES. | P. OFFICES. BY WHOM SUPPLIED. | NAMES OF DELEGATES. | Baptized. | Rec'd by Letter. | Restored. | Dis. by Letter. | Excluded. | Deceased. | Whites. | Colored. | Total Number. | Funds. £ ct. | Ch. Meetings. |
|---|---|---|---|---|---|---|---|---|---|---|---|---|---|---|
| Lick Creek, | Davidson, | Jackson Hill, A. Kinney, | Michael Redwine, John Redwine, Joseph Kerk, | 31 | | 1 | | | 1 | 79 | 3 | 82 | 2.00 | 4$ |
| Jersey, | Davidson, | Cotton Grove, Wm. Turner, | William Turner, John Wilson, James Wiseman, | 1 | | 5 | | | 3 | 117 | 144 261 | | 2.30 | 1$ |
| Abbott's Creek, | do | Abbott's Creek, B. Lanier, | Joseph Spurgen, D. Raper, John Teague, | 37 | | 2 | 1 | | 1 | 85 | | 85 | 1.15 | 3$ |
| Tom's Creek, | do | Healing Springs, B. Lanier, | B. Lanier, John Lanier, Peter Riley, | 2 | | 1 | | 1 | | 29 | 2 | 31 | 1.00 | 1$ |
| Jamestown, | Guilford, | Jamestown, N. Hertford, | N. Hertford, Joseph Chambers, Joel Moody, | 18 | 2 | 1 | | | | 25 | | 25 | 1.00 | 4$ |
| Liberty, | Davidson, | Fair Grove, B. Lanier, | G. W. Pope, Benjamin May, Zebulon Minor, | 7 | | | | | | 46 | 2 | 48 | 1.75 | 2$ |
| Holloways, | do | Silverhill, A. Kinney, | A. Palmer, George Cross, William Nusom, | 10 | 1 | 1 | | | 2 | 63 | 26 | 89 | 2.00 | 2$ |
| New Friendship, | Forsythe, | Salem, Wm. Turner, | John Charles, Alexander Delap, David Charles, | 4 | 1 | | 1 | 1 | | 30 | | 30 | 1.00 | 4$ |
| Big Creek, | Montgomery, | Wind Hill, B. Lanier, | Eli Davis, Eli Coggin, William Hamilton, | 4 | | 1 | 1 | 1 | | 43 | 4 | 47 | 75 | 4$ |
| Pine M. House, | Davidson, | Lexington, A. Williams, | Richard Barnes, sen'r., R. Barnes, Wm. Nunley, | 1 | | | 1 | 1 | | 18 | 1 | 19 | 1.00 | 3$ |
| Reed's X Roads, | do | do ........... | A. Williams, A. Yarbrough, J. A. Parks, J. Cornish. | | 2 | | 2 | 1 | | 53 | | 53 | 1.60 | 2$ |
| Marion, | do | do ........... | R. Witherington, J. Green, A. R. Witherington, | 2 | 1 | 1 | | | 1 | 26 | 3 | 29 | 50 | 4$ |
| Salisbury, | Rowan, | Salisbury, J. B. Solomon, | William Lambeth, John A. Weirman, | | 1 | | | 1 | 1 | 15 | | 15 | 50 | 4$ |
| | | | | 107 | 6 | 4 | 11 | 6 | 8 | 623 | 191 | 814 | 16.65 | |

A List of Ordained Preachers in this Association: A. Kinney, of Lick Creek; B. Lanier, of Tom's Creek; Wm. Turner, of the Jersey; and A. Williams, of Reed's X Roads.—Licentiates: Gm. Tussey, of Reed's X Roads; Robert Goaly, of Marion; Dempsey Parks of Lick Creek, and Z. Minor, of Liberty.

# MINUTES OF LIBERTY ASSOCIATION.

### THE NINETEETH ANNIVERSARY

OF

## THE LIBERTY ASSOCIATION,

WAS HELD AT LIBERTY CHURCH, DAVIDSON COUNTY, N. C.,
August 22d., 23d., and 24th., 1851.

1. Introductory Sermon was delivered by brother Wm. Turner, from Luke 19th chapter, 10th verse.

2. The Association was organized by brother B. Lanier, acting as Moderator.

3. After singing and prayer, by bro. Benjamin Lanier, letters from the Churches were read, contents noted. (See last page.) The Association then proceeded by ballot to elect brother William Turner, Moderator for the present term.

4. Opened the way for corresponding brethren. Bro. Amos Weaver, from the Yadkin; bro. B. H. Carter, from the Pee Dee; J. J. James, from the Beulah, came forward, and were received and invited to take seats with us.

5. On motion, invited Ministering brethren to take seats. Bro. B. Lanier accepted the invitation.

6. On motion, proceeded to appoint brethren B. Lanier, A. Kinney, B. May, Jesse Styers, and John Teague, with the Moderator and Clerk, a Committee of Arrangements.

7. Appointed brethren J. Welch, and A. R. Craver, a Committee of Finance.

8. Appointed brethren Benj. Lanier, J. H. Crouch, Quilla Jones, a Committee on Church Letters and state of Religion.

9. Appointed W. N. Herriford, Jefferson Charles, Jesse H. Owen, a Committee on Sabbath Schools.

10. Appointed brethren J. J. James, B. H. Carter, and Wm. Owen, on Missions.

11. Appointed brethren, A. Williams, J. J. James, and A. Weaver, on Education.

12. On motion, agreed to give place to the Bible Society on Saturday, at three o'clock.

13. Committees are to report on Saturday, if convenient, if not on Monday.

14. On motion, appointed the Moderator and Clerk, with the Delegates of the Church, a Committee to arrange preaching during the meeting, except the Sabbath.

15. On motion, adjourned until Saturday, nine o'clock. Prayer by bro. Amos Weaver.

---

SATURDAY, AUGUST 23, 1851.

Met according to adjournment. Prayer by brother A. Williams.

1. On motion, the Report of the Committee of Arrangements. Received.

2. On motion, the Committee on Missions reported. Report received and Committee discharged. (See letter A.)

3. The Committee on Church Letters and state of Religion reported. Report received and Committee discharged. (See appendix B.)

4. Correspondents to sister Associations were called on to report, which was done as far as present, and gave encouraging accounts of those that were attended. Those brethren that failed were excused.

5. On motion, the Association then proceeded to appoint correspondents to sister Associations, when the following appointments were made: To the Yadkin, to commence the Saturday before the first Sabbath in October, at Grassy Knob, Richard Barnes, Jr., J. H. Owen, A. R. Craver. Brier Creek, J. Styers, Wm. Owen, to embrace the fourth Sabbath in September. To Sandy Creek, J. H. Crouch, B. May, to commence on Friday before the first Sabbath in October. To Pee Dee, Eli Davis, G. F. Smith, to commence on Friday before the fourth Sabbath in September. To the Beulah, to commence on Friday before the third Sabbath in August, 1852, bro's. B. Lanier, Wm. Turner, A. Williams.

6. On motion, proceeded to elect by ballot, brethren J. J. James, A. Weaver, Wm. Turner, to occupy the stand on the Sabbath, and preach a Missionary Sermon, at 11 o'clock.

7. Bro. W. N. Herriford reported that he performed something like a month's service as a Missionary within the bounds of the Association.

The Association proceeded to take up a collection to pay him, and received between four and five dollars.

Called for an hour.

Resumed business again.

8. Committee of Finance reported that they had received from the Churches eighteen dollars and fifty eight cents.

9. Treasurer reported that there was a deficiency of one dollar and eighty-five cents from last year.

10. The Committee on Education reported and was discharged. (See letter C.)

11. On motion, appointed one delegate from each Church as a Committee to consider the propriety of having missionary next, and report on Monday. A. Kinney, William Owen, J. Spurgen, John Lanier, J. Welch, B. May, A. Palmer, J. Styers, E. C. Coggin, R. Barns, Jr., A. Williams, A. R. Witherington, John R. Owen, Wm. Turner.

12. On motion, adjourned until Monday 9 o'clock, and gave place to the Bible Society, to hold its meeting. Prayer by bro. J. J. James.

## SABBATH.

The brethren appointed to occupy the stand, met a large congregation. Elder Amos Weaver, from the Yadkin, occupied the stand at 10 o'clock; and preached from Titus, 3d chapter and 5th verse. Elder William Turner, from 1 Cor. 16th chapter and 22d verse. Elder J. J. James, from Luke 2, and 10th verse. The congregation was large and attentive, the word preached seemed blessed to the edifying of christians and convincing to sinners.

MONDAY, AUGUST 25, 1851.

1. Met according to adjournment. Prayer by brother Herriford.

2. On motion, Committee on Sabbath Schools reported, and were dismissed. (See letter D.)

2. On motion, agreed to meet on Saturday instead of Friday, and continue in session until all the business is finished.

4. On motion, agreed to hold the next annual meeting of this body with Halloway's Church, to commence on Saturday before the fourth Sabbath in August next.

5. Appointed bro. A. Kinney to preach the Introductory Sermon, and bro. W. N. Herriford, his alternate.

6. On motion, the collection taken up on Sabbath amounting to seven dollars and eighty cents, is to remain in the hands of the Treasurer until called on by this body to pay a Missionary.

7. On motion, and after it was duly considered, the following resolution was unanimously adopted by the Association :

*Whereas,* much excitement has lately prevailed in this part of the community on the subject of abolitionism, and whereas a certain religious sect calling themselves true Wesleyans, are said to entertain abolition sentiments, therefore,

*Resolved,* That this Association disclaim all connection or sympathy with said society, and the Churches are hereby recommended not to allow any abolitionist to preach in any of our houses of worship.

8. The Committee on Missions reported favorably to Missions. Report received and Committee discharged.

9. The Presbytery of the Association reported the ordination of bro. Wm. N. Herriford, to the work of the Ministry.

10. On motion, agreed that we have no Missionary this year.

11. On motion,

*Resolved,* That we recognize all of the ordained Ministers of our Associations as members *ex-officio,* and we order the Clerk to prepare an article to be attached to the Constitution to that effect.

12. *Whereas,* the question was asked whether the Church has the right to judge whether confidence was necessary in an excluded member, On motion, we answer, yes.

*Resolved,* That the sincere thanks of this Association be tendered to the brethren and friends for their kindness in supporting the meeting during this session.

After singing and prayer by Wm. Turner, this Association adjourned to the time and place above named.

WILLIAM TURNER, Moderator.

AZARIAH WILLIAMS, *Clerk.*

Your Committee on Missions, having had the subject under consideration, offer the following report :

When Christ had finished his work on earth for the salvation of man, and was about to go back to heaven, he sent out his Apostles, and commissioned them to "go into all the world and preach the gospel to every creature," promising to be with them by his spirit "even to the end of the world." This command which he gave them was intended for the Church through all coming time ; and makes it obligatory on us to do what we can to extend the preaching of the Gospel in destitute portions of our own land, and also in heathen countries. The work of Missions is now divided into two departments, Home and Foreign ; or the supplying the destitute in our own country, and the sending of Missionaries to labor for the conversion of the heathen.

Our State Convention is engaged in sustaining missions in both of these departments. We have brethren preaching as missionaries in different destitute sections of our State, and their reports furnish interesting accounts of the numbers they have baptized and the new Churches which they have built up ; but much yet remains to be done. There are yet many destitute places that need the Word of Life. Within the bounds of this Association a Missionary might find much to do, and your Committee are fully persuaded that one ought to be employed to labor within its bounds.

In regard to the Foreign Field, we are doing but little comparatively, for the salvation of the heathen. When we consider that more than one half of the human race are still in heathenish darkness, and that only a few missionaries have been sent to enlighten them in the knowledge of God, how solemn is the responsibility which rests upon us to do more to send them the Gospel. Brother and sister Yates, who went out a few years ago to labor in Shanghai, China, are still doing what they can at that important post. Let us not forget to remember them in our supplications at a throne of grace, that the Lord may give them success in teaching the heathen a knowledge of his will.

Your Committee would recommend the Churches, composing this

body, to keep up a connection with our State Convention by appointing delegates and sending up funds to sustain our Missionary operations.

All of which is respectfully submitted.

---

## B.

## REPORT ON CHURCH LETTERS AND STATE OF RELIGION.

---

The Committee to whom was referred the examining of Church Letters and state of Religion within the bounds of this Association, report dear brethren, we are of the opinion from the statements of the Churches in their letters to this body, that coldness and lukewarmness pervades most, if not all the Churches within our bounds, and also from the fact that there has been few accessions to our Churches during the last year. Brethren, we recommend the following remedies for the above named evil. First, that the Churches in this Association hold prayer meetings at their places of public worship, and other convenient places. Second, we recommend the appointment of some brother to ride as missionary within our bounds, and stir up our brethren to a lively zeal upon the subject of missions ; and also upon revivals of religion, in order that our Churches may once more flourish, and the cause of the Redeemer's Kingdom advance in the world.

All of which is respectfully submitted,

BENJAMIN LANIER, Chairman.

---

## C.

## EDUCATION.

---

The Committee on Education offer the following Report :

Among the various improvements of the present age, there are none that have advanced more rapidly than the cause of Education. It is pleasing to witness the interest which is now taken by many parents in the proper instruction of their children. The education of the rising generation is one of the most important subjects which can engage the attention of all who love their country and their race. It gives to an individual an influence which nothing else can impart. A young man or woman with a good education may soon acquire influence, and do much more to benefit society than one with a large fortune but uneducated. But it is particularly in reference to our denominal interests that we are called upon now to consider education, and your Committee would call attention to Wake Forest College, as a Baptist Institution for education. The College is now in a more promising condition than it has ever been before. It is well filled with students, and is sending out an influence every year in favor of our denomination. It ought to be still more extensively patronized; and it would do much more for our cause.

Your Committee are also gratified to state that since the last meeting of this body, an Institution has been established for Female Education, to be under the control and management of our denomination. This School is known as the Oxford Female College, and located in the Town of Oxford, Granville County. It is to be carried on upon an extensive scale, and deserves the patronage and support of Baptists. As a denomination, we ought to support our own Institutions. By sending to other schools, the Baptists have lost much in money, and much in influence. All of which is respectfully submitted.

------

## D.

### REPORT ON SABBATH SCHOOLS.

Your Committee beg leave to report, that they have had the matter under consideration; they think it important that the young be instructed in the Holy Scriptures, and that the institution of Sabbath Schools is calculated to do good in this way. They regret to say that there seems not to be that interest taken in the matter that would be desired. It seems, however, that two or three of the Churches have irregular Sabbath Schools which are doing some good. May the Great Head of the Church assist them. Respectfully submitted,

WM. N. HERRIFORD, Chairman.

# TABLE OF CONTENTS.

| CHURCHES. | COUNTIES. | P. OFFICES. | BY WHOM SUPPLIED. | NAMES OF DELEGATES. | Baptized | Rec'd by Letter | Restored | Dis. by Letter | Excluded | Deceased | Whites | Colored | Total Numbers | Funds | Ch. Meetings |
|---|---|---|---|---|---|---|---|---|---|---|---|---|---|---|---|
| Lick Creek, | Davidson, | Jackson Hill, | A. Kinney, | A. Kinney, G. F. Smith, and Michael Redwine, | 16 | 1 | | 3 | 2 | | 91 | 3 | 94 | 2 00 | 1S |
| Jersey, | Davidson, | Cotton Grove, | Wm. Turner, | Wm. Turner, Mathias Long, and William Owen, | 1 | | | 10 | 3 | 1 | 110 | 135 | 245 | 2 72 | 3S |
| Abbott's Creek, | do, | Abbott's Creek, | Wm. Turner, | Joseph Spurgen, Quilla Jones, John Teague, | 9 | 1 | | 5 | 2 | 1 | 86 | | 86 | 2 00 | 3S |
| Tom's Creek, | do, | Healing Springs, | B. Lanier, | Peter Riley, John Skein, John Lanier, | 1 | | | 1 | | | 30 | | 30 | 1 00 | 4S |
| Jamestown, | Guilford, | Jamestown, | W. Herriford, | W. N. Herriford, J. Welch, J. H. Crouch, | 7 | 6 | | 6 | 8 | 1 | 25 | | 25 | 1 25 | 4S |
| Liberty, | Davidson, | Fair Grove, | Z. Miner, | Henry Fouts, B. May, Richard Beckerdite, | 14 | 1 | | 3 | 21 | 1 | 56 | 2 | 58 | 1 30 | 2S |
| Holloways, | do, | Silver Hill, | A. Kinney, | George Cross, John Cross, Abraham Palmer, | | | 1 | | | 2 | 52 | 32 | 84 | 1 70 | 2S |
| New Friendship, | Forsythe, | Salem, | Wm. Turner, | John Charles, Jefferson Charles, Jesse Styers, | | | | | | | 28 | | 28 | 75 | 2S |
| Big Creek, | Montgomery, | Wind Hill, | B. Lanier, | Eli Coggin, E. H. Davis, Wm. Hamilton, | 1 | | | 1 | 1 | | 43 | 4 | 47 | 70 | 4S |
| Pine M. House, | Davidson, | Lexington, | A. Williams, | Richard Barnes, Sr., Richard Barnes, Jr., | 1 | 4 | | | 1 | | 11 | | 11 | 1 21 | 3S |
| Reed's X Roads, | do, | do, | A. Williams, | Jesse H. Owen, A. R. Craver, A. Williams, | 4 | | | 3 | 1 | | 52 | | 52 | 1 50 | 4S |
| Marion, | do, | do, | R. Goaly, | R. Goaly, A. R. Witherington, Jesse Green, | 4 | 4 | | 4 | | | 22 | 3 | 25 | 65 | 4S |
| Salisbury, | Rowan, | Salisbury, | J. B. Solomon, | Wm. Lambeth, A. G. Allen, J. R. Owen, | 12 | 14 | | | | | 31 | 10 | 41 | 2 00 | 3S |
| | | | | Total, | 64 | 22 | | 24 | 26 | 9 | 637 | 190 | 827 | 18.58 | |

*A List of Ordained Preachers in this Association:* A. Kinney, of Lick Creek; B. Lanier, of Tom's Creek; Wm. Turner, of the Jersey; A. Williams, of Reed's X Roads, and Wm. N. Herriford, of Jameston. *Licentiates:* Gm. Tussey, R. Goaly, Dempsy Parks; Z. Miner, J. H. Crouch, and John Teague.

# MINUTES

OF THE

## TWENTY-FIRST SESSION

OF THE

# LIBERTY BAPTIST ASSOCIATION,

HELD AT

## ABBOTT'S CREEK MEETING HOUSE,

DAVIDSON COUNTY, N. C.,

AUGUST 27—29, 1853.

SALISBURY, N. C.:
MILLER & JAMES, PRINTERS.

1853.

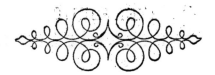

# PROCEEDINGS OF LIBERTY ASSOCIATION.

———o———

ABBOTT'S CREEK MEETING HOUSE, DAVIDSON COUNTY, }
August 27, 1853.

THE members of the Liberty Association met according to adjournment, when the Introductory Sermon was preached by brother B. Lanier, from Mat. 24th ch., and 14th v.

1. After a short intermission, the members met again, and the Association was called to order by our former Moderator. Religious exercises were conducted by bro. Wm. Turner.

2. The Churches were then called by the Moderator, when their letters were presented and their contents noted. (See last page.)

3. Finding that a majority of the Delegates from the Churches present, the Association proceeded to the choice of a Moderator for the present term, which resulted in the election of B. Lanier.

On motion of bro. Wm. Turner, the Moderator called on correspondents from sister Associations and invited them to take seats, when bro.'s John Robeson, T. S. Yarbrough, R. Goaley, Wm. N. Herriford, Julius Terrell, H. J. Robeson, and Orin Churchill, from the Beulah, and C. W. Bessent, J. J. Blackwood, from the Yadkin; Enoch Crutchfield, from the Sandy Creek, all came forward, were cordially received by the Moderator giving the hand of fellowship.

On motion, invitation given to Ministering Brethren.

4. On motion, appointed bro.'s William Turner, Joseph Spurgen, William Coggin, with the Moderator and Clerk, a Committee of Arrangements, with the invitation to Corresponding Ministers to set with them.

5. On motion of bro. Robeson a committee was appointed to arrange preaching during the meeting, consisting of the Pastor and Delegates of Abbott's Church and bro. Wm. Turner, and to appoint some bro. to preach a Missionary Sermon on Sabbath at eleven o'clock, A. M.

6. On motion of bro. Wm. Turner, that a collection be taken up on Sabbath, and that the same be appropriated to Missionary purposes within the bounds of this Association.

7. On motion, bro. John Teague and John Redwine were appointed a Committee of Finance.

8. On motion of bro. Griffiith, the following Committees were appointed, viz:

On *Sabbath Schools*—R. H. Griffith, C. W. Bessent, and J. Welch.

On *Missions*—T. S. Yarbrough, Peter Riley, and A. Delap.

On *Education*—William Lambeth, R. H. Griffith, and Richard Barnes, Sr.

On *Church Letters and state of Religion*—Bro. Wm. Turner, Wm. N. Herriford, R. Jacobs, John Teague.

On *State Convention*—Bro. Wm. Turner, T. S. Teague, R. Jacobs, and A. Palmer.

8. On motion, the Association give place to the Bible Society on Monday at twelve o'clock to hold their meeting.

On motion, that all papers be referred to the Committee of Arrangements, with letter from Wm. H. Hamner.

On motion, adjourned until Monday nine o'clock. Benediction bro. by R. H. Griffith.

# SABBATH.

THE brethren appointed to occupy the stand, at the appointed hours met a large and orderly congregation, and preached as follows, to wit:

Elder C. W. Bessent, at 8 o'clock, A. M., from 9th chap. of John and 4th verse.

' Elder R. H. Griffith, at 10 o'clock, from 3d chap. of John and 16th verse.

Elder T. S. Yarbrough, at 10 o'clock, from 14th chapter of Matthew and 19th verse.

Elder E. Crutchfield, at two o'clock, P. M., from 18th chapter of Proverbs and 19th verse.

Elder Wm. N. Herriford, at night, from 4th chapter of Collossians and 2d verse.

The word preached had a good effect on those that heard.

---

*Monday Morning,* 9 *o'clock.*

MET according to adjournment. Prayer by bro. John Robeson.

1. On motion of bro. R. H. Griffith, the report of the Committee of arrangements was received and dismissed.

2. Called on Correspondents to report. Those appointed to Yadkin reported: attended and had an interesting meeting. Those appointed to the other Associations failed to attend. Only one attended the Peedee.

3. On motion the following Correspondents were appointed to sister Associations:

*To the Yadkin*—John Teague, Richard R. Griffith, William Turner.

*To the Brier Creek*—On motion of bro. Turner, that the Clerk correspond with them by forwarding them a package of our Minutes.

*To the Sandy Creek, first Sabbath in October*—Joel Moody, Jonathan Welch, and Azariah Williams.

*To the Pee Dee.*—Enoch Davis, Eli Davis.

*To the Beulah.*—Richard H. Griffith, Wm. Turner, A. Delap, and B. Lanier.

4. On motion, our Missionary, bro. R. Jacks, reported. Report received. (See Letter B.)

5. On motion, Committees reported, and reports adopted. (See Letter C, on Education; Letter D, on Missions; Letter E, on the Baptist State Convention; Letter F, on the State of Religion, and Church Letters, A.

The Committee on Finance reported as follows:

| Churches. | Missionary Fund. | Association Fund. |
|---|---|---|
| Lick Creek, | $6 87½ | $1 75 |
| Jersey, | | 2 80 |
| Abbott's Creek, | 2 75 | 2 00 |
| Marion, | 2 00 | 55 |
| Liberty, | | 1 00 |
| Holloway's, (by A. Palmer,) | 5 00 | 1 65 |
| Big Creek, | 3 00 | 1 00 |
| Reed's ⋈ Roads, | 8 75 | 1 70 |
| Pine M. House, | | 1 00 |
| Tom's Creek, | 6 00 | 75 |
| Jamestown, | 3 10 | 75 |
| New Friendship, | 7 50 | 1 00 |
| Salisbury, | | 1 50 |
| | 44 97½ | 17 45 |
| Public collection on Sabbath, | 19 30  Due Clerk, | 25 |
| | 64 27½ | 17 20 |

The balance due the Missionary, was paid by the following individuals:

| | | | |
|---|---|---|---|
| Joseph Spurgen, | $2 00 | Wm. Raper, Sr., | $0 50 |
| R. Witherington, | 1 00 | R. S. Green, | 50 |
| H. Copple, | 1 00 | T. S. Yarbrough, | 50 |
| Joel Moody, | 1 00 | R. H. Griffith, | 50 |
| | Jacob Huffman, 50, | | |

And different brethren paid the balance.

6. On motion, the Treasurer was authorised to pay the same over to the Missionary.

7. On motion, bro. Richard Jacks was appointed Missionary for the ensuing year, to ride the whole year at $20 per month, amounting to $240 per year.

8. On motion, appointed a Board of Missions, consisting of one member from each Church, to manage the Missionary operations in the Association, consisting of Wm. Turner, John Redwine, Joseph Spurgen, B. Lanier, Jonathan

Welch, Henry Copple, A. Williams, A. Palmer, David Charles, Wm. R. Coggin, Richard Barnes, Sr., R. S. Green, A. G. Allen, and any five of that number to form a quorum.

9. On motion agreed to hold the next Annual Meeting of this body with Reed ⋈ Roads Church, five miles west of Lexington, to commence on Friday before the fourth Sabbath in August, 1854.

10. On motion, appointed bro. A. Kinney to preach the Introductory Sermon, and bro. Wm. Turner, his alternate.

11. On motion, appointed bro. Richard H. Griffith, to preach the Missionary Sermon on Sabbath at 11 o'clock, and bro. Lanier his alternate.

12. On motion, appointed the ordained Ministers of this Association a standing Presbytery for this year, and three of them to form a quorum.

13. *Whereas*, There is disorder existing in the Church at New Friendship, we agree to appoint a Committee of seven to attend them on Saturday before the second Lord's day in October next, and to report to the next Association what members are living in peace, and who they consider the Church. The Committee to consist of A. Palmer, Aquilla Jones, Jonathan Welch, William Clinard, Joseph Spurgen, Jesse Jones, George F. Smith, and on motion, bro. R. Jacks, our Missionary, was appointed to attend at the same time.

14. On motion, *Resolved*, That this Association observe Friday before the first Sabbath in November, as a day of Thanksgiving and Prayer to Almighty God for a Revival of Religion within these bounds and throughout the world.

15. On motion, *Resolved*, That this Association return thanks to the brethren and friends for their hospitality in entertaining the members of the Association during its session.

Received of Azariah Williams, Treasurer, Eighty Dollars in full for Missionary labor rendered in the bounds of Liberty Association, the past year.
August 30, 1853.                                                R. JACKS.

On motion, *Resolved,* That this Association recommend the patronage of the Biblical Recorder and the Home and Foreign Journal.

A memorial presented to the Association on Saturday and referred to the Committee of Arrangements, was now read before the Association. After some remarks by several brethren, the following preamble and resolutions were offered and unanimously adopted, bro. Richard H. Griffith, acting as Clerk, *pro. tem.*

*Whereas,* Wm. H. Hamner has presented a memorial to this body in which he charges the Baptist Church at Reed's Cross Roads with unchristian conduct in its refusal to restore him to its fellowship, therefore

*Resolved,* That we see no cause for disapproving the course by the Church in this matter, and still retain full confidence in its impartiality and gospel order.

*Whereas,* The character of bro. A. Williams, has been publicly impeached by William H. Hamner, charging him with falsehood, therefore

*Resolved,* That we have implicit confidence in the veracity and piety of bro. A. Williams. RICHARD H. GRIFFITH, Clerk, *pro tem.*

All the Delegates names marked thus *, were absent.
Test. BENJ. LANIER, *Moderator.*
A. WILLIAMS, *Secretary.*

## Missionary Board.

THE Board appointed on Missionary operations within this Association, will hold Quarterly Meetings in the Town of Lexington, commencing on Staturday before the 4th Sabbath in November next, to transact the business belonging to said Board. A full attendance is desired every time if possible. BENJ. LANIER, *Chairman.*
A. WILLIAMS, *Secretary.*

# Appendix.

---

## A
# Report of Committee on Church Letters & State of Religion.

---o---

YOUR Committee submit the following report:—They have ascertained that in some sections within our bounds, there is a good state of feeling. In the neighborhoods of Liberty, Toms Creek, Reed's ⋈ Roads, Abbott's Creek and Salisbury, God has been pouring out his Spirit, and many have turned to the ways of righteousness. The Churches seem to be at peace among themselves, but some of them are destitute of pastoral supplies. There is much room, also, for ministerial labor in destitute neighborhoods; an efficient Missionary has great room to do good, both in acting as pastor of destitute Churches, and in preaching the Gospel of Jesus Christ in destitute neighborhoods. May the Great Head of the Church assist us to do his will.

WILLIAM TURNER.

---

## B
# Missionary Report.

---o---

DEAR BRETHREN:—It now becomes my duty to report to you some amount of labor as your Missionary. I have had some good meetings. The Lord has blessed his own Truth in the conviction of sinners; saints have been made happy in the Love of God, and forwarded on their journey towards heaven. At some of my meetings we witnessed several happy conversions. Our missionary operations are advancing in the bounds of the Association, there are some difficulties in the way. But these can be surmounted. Let us thank God for what he has done, and persevere in the good work, trusting his grace for time to come.' I have travelled 126 days, preached 98 sermons, baptized one, and '13 have professed hope in Christ. At my meetings we have made collections for the Association, which funds were sent up by their delegates. All of which is respectfully submitted. R. JACKS.

---

## C

## Report of the Committee on Sabbath Schools.

----o----

YOUR Committee beg leave to report, that the great field of christian effort at the present day, in our land, is the youthful mind. It is the one most promising of success—yet the one most neglected. In youth, the mind is most susceptible of impressions—impressions that last during life, giving tone to the character, and shaping the destiny of the individual. Now, shall there be in this season of youth no religious impressions? Shall not the youthful mind —ay, the youthful heart be pointed to the Savior who said, "suffer little children to come unto me"?

In the view of your Committee, the Sabbath School is the very best plan to effect results so desirable. The history of the Sabbath School shows this.— Any Church that wishes to do any thing for the religious welfare of the rising generation, should have and keep up a Sabbath School. Therefore,

*Resolved*, That we, Delegates and Ministers, here assembled in Association, will do all we possibly can to start and keep up a Sabbath School in the Churches to which we belong, and which we here represent.

RICHARD H. GRIFFITH, *Chairman.*

---

## D

## Report of the Committee on Education.

----o----

IT is the opinion of your Committee, that no parent discharges the obligations God has imposed upon him or her, who fails to use every possible means to give to his or her children a good education. The day of ignorance is rapidly passing away, the day of general knowledge is already dawning upon us, and the youth who is deprived of the advantages of education will be—must be behind the age. He will feel it in after life; he will be less useful than he could be with a well improved mind, while he will lose a vast amount of pleasure which can be drawn alone from the store house of knowledge. Nor is this all. The parent should be careful that the seeds of truth should be sown

in early life... The seeds of error may be planted in the youthful mind without any direct effort so to do, but simply from the influence of association,
and the example of those to whom they look as models.   Therefore,

*Resolved,* That we recommend to every parent within the bounds of this Association, that they give their children a good education, and that in effecting
this, they encourage such schools as are free from the influence of what we
believe to be error—in other words that they patronize Baptist Schools.   All
of which is respectfully submitted.

WILLIAM LAMBETH, Chairman.

## E
# Report on Missions.

——o——

YOUR Committee regard the cause of Missions as the cause of Christ.   They
look upon the great command of our Lord, when about to leave the earth, as our
authority for using our best efforts to send the Gospel to every creature under heaven,   We deem it highly conducive, and in some Associations absolutely necessary to the growth of our denomination, and the proper religious
instruction of many neighborhoods, that a Missionary or Missionaries be employed to labor within their bounds; nor do we suppose that our duty to send
the Gospel to the destitute of our State or country at all conflicts with that
of sending it to the lands of heathenism.   On the contrary, we believe Home
and Foreign Missions to be mutual stimulants to each other.   The same spirit that causes us to desire the conversion of our fellow countryman, prompts
us to desire the salvation of our fellow man wherever he may be found; and as
our efforts and zeal increases for the one, so they naturally will for the other.
We are happy to say that many of our Associations in this State are sustaining
and enjoying the services of one or more Missionaries within their bounds,
and we hope that ere long this will be the case in every Association throughout the State.   According to the last minutes of the N. Carolina Baptist State
Convention, that body has in its employ eight Missionaries laboring successfully
in different parts of the State.   The Southern Board of Foreign Missions has
in its employ about thirty Missionaries and Assistants, four from this State,
divided about equally between China and Africa.   These Missions are at present, by the mercy of God prosperous, and having been lately reinforced,
promise a rich reward.   Your Committee would earnestly exhort you to cherish the missionary spirit, and to testify your own value of the gospel by lib-
eral and willing sacrifices to send it to others who have it not.   All of which
is respectfully submitted.

T. G. YARBROUGH, Chairman.

# Report on the Baptist State Convention.

———o———

**F**

THIS body, formed of delegates from Baptist Churches in Eastern and Middle North Carolina, has existed in its present form about twenty-four years. Its object is to diffuse and excite a benevolent spirit among the Churches, and by union and combination of effort, to carry on more successfully the Missionary cause. Its funds, in general, are equally divided between Foreign and Home Missions and Education of the rising ministry.

Its funds appropriated to Foreign Missions, are applied to the use of the Foreign missionaries through the Foreign Board located in the city of Richmond, Va. Four Foreign Missionaries are from this State, brothers Lacy and Yates with their wives.

The Convention has usually in its employ about eight Home Missionaries, who have hitherto labored mostly in the Middle and Western portion of the State. The labors of the Missionaries have been greatly blessed, and many entire Churches have been built up by their instrumentality.

The young Ministers, assisted by the Convention in procuring an education, are generally six or seven in number, at present only four. This is one of the most important objects of the Convention, as the steady advance of our cause depends in a great manner on an intelligent and able ministry.

Your Committee feel happy in being able to recommend to you so favorable an opportunity of becoming acquainted and co-operating with the brethren throughout the State, and indeed throughout the whole South, as is presented to you in the State Convention. We would earnestly recommend every Church, therefore in this Association, to send one or more delegates to its meetings. Every Church or individual brother or sister that contributes ten dollars to its funds in one year is entitled to one delegate for that year. Thirty dollars constitutes a life member. All of which is respectfully submitted.

WILLIAM TURNER, *Chairman.*

# Tabular View of the Churches.

| CHURCHES. | COUNTIES. | P. OFFICES. | BY WHOM SUPPLIED. | NAMES OF DELEGATES. | Baptized | Rec'd by letter | Restored | Dis. by letter | Excluded | Deceased | Whites | Coloured | Total No. | Funds $ ct. | Ch. Meetings |
|---|---|---|---|---|---|---|---|---|---|---|---|---|---|---|---|
| Lick Creek, | Davidson, | Jackson Hill, | A. Kinney, | P. Redwine, Jo. Bean, John Redwine, | | | | | | 1 | 94 | 1 | 95 | 1 75 | 48 |
| Jersey, | do | Cotton Grove, | A. Weaver, | *A. Weaver, Geo. F. Smith, James Wiseman, | 10 | | | | 1 | 5 | 109 | 139 | 248 | 2 80 | 1 |
| Abbott's Creek, | do | Abbott's Creek, | Jno. Robeson, | Wm. Raper, Jos. Spurgen, John Teague, | | 1 | | 1 | | 2 | 84 | | 84 | | 3 |
| Tom's Creek, | do | Healing Springs, | B. Lanier, | John Lanier, Peter Riley, Simeon Sheets, | | | | | 2 | | 20 | 4 | 24 | | 4 |
| Jamestown, | Guilford, | Jamestown, | W. J. Witherington, | J. Welch, Joel Moody, *J. Greenwood, | 2 | 1 | | | | 1 | 49 | 1 | 50 | | 1 |
| Liberty, | Davidson, | Fair Grove, | B. Lanier, | H. Copple, B. May, N. Jarratt, | | | | | 6 | 3 | 53 | 29 | 82 | | 52 |
| Holloway's, | do | Silver Hill, | A. Kinney, | J. Huffman, *Wm. Newsom, A. Palmer, | | | | | | | 29 | | 29 | | 28 |
| New Friendship, | Forsythe, | Salem, | A. Kinney, | A. Delap. Jo. Thomas, D. Charles, | | | | | | | 45 | 3 | 48 | | 3 |
| Big Creek, | Montgomery, | Wind Hill, | B. Lanier, | Wm. R. Coggin, E. H. Davis, *Eli Davis, | | | | | | 1 | 11 | | 11 | | 3 |
| Pine M. House, | Davidson, | Lexington, | B. Lanier, | R. Barnes, Sr., *R. Barnes, Jr., | 15 | 1 | | | | | 68 | | 68 | | 2 |
| Reed's X Roads, | do | do | A. Williams, | *A. Yarbrough, A. R. Craver, B. Myers, | 2 | | | | | | 17 | 3 | 20 | | 2 |
| Marion, | do | do | B. Lanier, | R. Witherington, J. Green, R. S. Green, | 12 | 4 | | | | | 46 | 11 | 57 | | 2 |
| Salisbury, | Rowan, | Salisbury, | R. H. Griffith, | R. H. Griffith, Wm. Lambeth, A. G. Allen, | | | | | | | 21 | | 21 | | 2 |
| | | | | | 54 | 7 | | 6 | 11 | 12 | 646 | 191 | 837 | 17 45 | |

*Ordained Preachers.*—A. Kinney, B. Lanier, A. Williams, Wm. Turner, R. H. Griffith. *Licentiates.*—Gm. Tussey, D. Parks, A. Yarbrough.

# MINUTES

OF THE

## TWENTY-SECOND SESSION

OF THE

# LIBERTY BAPTIST ASSOCIATION,

HELD AT

## REED'S ✕ ROADS MEETING HOUSE,

DAVIDSON COUNTY, N. C.,

*August 25, 26, 27, 28, 1854.*

MILLER & JAMES, PRINTERS,

SALISBURY, N. C.

1854.

# PROCEEDINGS

## OF

## LIBERTY ASSOCIATION.

———————◆———————

REED'S ⋈ ROADS MEETING HOUSE, DAVIDSON }
COUNTY, August 25, 1854. }

THE MEMBERS OF THE LIBERTY ASSOCIATION met according to adjournment, when the Introductory Sermon was preached by brother ALFRED KINNEY, from Luke the 15th chapter and 17th verse.

1. After a short intermission, the members met again, the Association was called to order by brother A. Kinney, the former Moderator being absent. Religious exercises were conducted by brother A. Kinney.

2. The Churches were then called to order by brother A. Kinney, (acting Moderator *pro tem.*,) when their letters were presented and their contents noted. (See last page.)

3. The Delegates present proceeded to the choice of a Moderator for the present term, which resulted in the election of brother Joseph Spurgen.

4. Called on Correspondents from sister Associations, and invited them to seats, when S. R. Varker, from Sandy Creek; C. W. Bessent, from the Yadkin; B. H. Carter, M.

Jones, F. M. Jordan, from Pee Dee; B. F. Eaton, from the Yadkin, E. Crutchfield, Sandy Creek, and W. C. Patterson, the Agent for the Publication Society, came forward and were cordially received.

On motion, ministering brethren invited to take seats, when brother Hugh McAlpin, from the Union Association came forward, and was received by the Moderator extending the right hand of fellowship.

On motion, appointed brethren A. Kinney, Wm. Owen, A. Delap, R. Wethrington, with the Clerk and Moderator, a Committee of Arrangements, and J. A. Carnigh, J. R. Nichols, a Committee of Finance.

On motion, a Committee was appointed to arrange preaching during the meeting, consisting of the Delegates and Pastor of the Church, with brother Wm. Owen and Joseph Kirk, R. Witherington.

4. On motion, adjourned until Saturday nine o'clock, A. M. Prayer by brother H. McAlpin.

---

*Saturday Morning*, 9 *o'clock.*

Met according to adjournment. Prayer by brother E. Crutchfield.

1. On motion, the Committee of Arrangements reported. The report was received and Committee continued.

2. Called on Correspondents to sister Associations to report. Those who attended were well received.

3. On motion, the following Correspondents were appointed to sister Associations.

*To the Yadkin*—John a Cornish, A. Williams, A. Delap, to be held at Swaim's Creek, to commence on Friday before the first Sabbath in October.

*To the Brier Creek*—On motion, as the distance is so great, we agree to keep up a correspondence by Minutes forwarded by the Clerk.

*To Sandy Creek*—First Sabbath in October, at Mount Pleasant Meeting House, brethren B. Lanier, J. Spurgen, William R. Coggin.

*To the Pee Dee*—To commence on Friday before the fourth Sabbath in September, brethren James Wiseman, Enoch Davis, Joseph Hamilton and William Crowder.

*To the Beulah*—Brethren Jas. Greenwood, John Teague, William Lambeth.

4. On motion, the following Committees were appointed.

*On Sabbath Schools*—B. Lanier, Wm. R. Coggin, F. M. Jordan.

*On Missions*—A. Williams, Wm. Turner, H. McAlpin.

*On Education*—Wm. C. Patterson, A. Kinney, William Lambeth.

*On Church Letters and State of Religion*—Brethren W. Owen, E. Crutchfield and B. Lanier.

*On State Convention*—Wm. C. Patterson, Wm. Turner, B. H. Carter.

*On Bible and Publication Society*—Wm. C. Patterson, Jesse Jones, Gm. Tussey.

5. Called off for one hour.

Resumed business again, when brother Denson A. Poindexter came forward as a Correspondent from the Yadkin, and was received by the Moderator extending the right hand of fellowship.

6. Committee of Finance reported that they had received from the Churches, $16 54

Found in the hands of the Treasurer, 95

Report received and Committee discharged.

7. Bro. Richard Jacks reported that he had rode one and

a half months and preached thirty-seven sermons; for which he charges the Association thirty-dollars, and which was paid in the following manner, viz:

| | |
|---|---|
| For Marion, by R. Withrington, - - -| $3 50 |
| " Abbott's Creek, by J. Spurgen, J. Jones, | 3 50 |
| " Lick Creek—M. Redwine, - - - | 3 50 |
| " Friendship—J. A. Nichols, - - - | 3 5C |
| " Tom's Creek—B. Lanier, P. Riley, - - | 2 75 |
| " Liberty—H. Copple, - - - - - | 2 50 |
| " Reed's—Gm. Tussey, - - - - | 5 00 |
| " Salisbury—A. G. Allen and Wm. Lambeth, | 2 45 |
| | $26 70 |
| The balance paid of Missionary fund, | 3 30 |
| | $30 00 |

8. On motion, agreed to hold the next annual meeting of this body with Lick Creek Church, south of Lexington 20 miles, to commence on Friday before the fourth Sabbath in August, 1855.

9. On motion, appointed bro. Wm. Turner to preach the Introductory Sermon, and bro. B. Lanier, his Alternate.

10. On motion, appointed bro. Wm. Turner to preach a Sermon on Charity, and bro. A. Kinney, his Alternate.

11. On motion, the Association gave place to the Bible and Publication Society on Monday at 11 o'clock, A. M.

12. On motion, adjourned until Monday 9 o'clock A. M.

Prayer by William Turner.

---

## SABBATH.

The brethren appointed to occupy the stand, preached. B. Lanier, 1st John 4—19 verses. "We lov... ...because he first loved us." Wm. C. Patterson, Isa. 60th chapter, 1 verse. Hugh McAlpin, from Luke 19th chapter verse 13, E. Crutchfield, from these words, "It pleased the Father that in him all fullness should dwell."

All was satisfactory—the congregation was large and serious—the word preached seemed blessed to the edification of saints, and to the awakening the impenitent.

---

*Monday Morning, 9 o'clock.*

Met according to adjournment. Singing and prayer by Elder A. Weaver.

On motion, bro. McAlpin was chosen assistant clerk.

1. On motion, the Committee appointed last year to visit the Friendship Church, be called upon to report.

2. On motion the case was recommitted to the same Committee.

3. On motion of bro. Turner, the Committee of Arrangements reported and Committee discharged.

4. On motion, the Committee on Missions reported. Report received and committee dismissed :

## REPORT ON MISSIONS,

Your Committee on Missions, beg leave to report that they consider the Missionary operations one of the most important objects of this body, from the fact that there is not that knowledge of Christ and his Gospel as is necessary. But the question arises how are we to carry out this great object? Certainly not by saying be ye clothed and fed, and lend no helping hand, but by acting as though you were in earnest. Let us remember that all we have of this world's goods are only loaned to us, and we are to use them not exclusively for ourselves, but for the advancement of the Redeemer's kingdom. Remember brethren, the Lord loves the cheerful giver. Brethren, we must be up and doing; the Lord has a work for us to do; we cannot stand in the desk and preach, but by our substance we can preach through those we may send forth. May God help us to be what we profess to be, (to wit,)

Baptists. A volume might be written on this subject, but we speak as unto wise men, and it is said that a word to the wise is sufficient. May the Lord enlarge our hearts, and make us willing to do much more for the cause of our Lord than ever. All of which is respectfully submitted.

A. WILLIAMS, Chairman.

The Committee on Sabbath Schools reported and were discharged:

### REPORT ON SABBATH SCHOOLS.

Your Committee on Sabbath Schools are of the opinion that there is but little interest taken in this glorious enterprize within the bounds of this Association, from the fact that there is but one School under our patronage within our limits. Dear brethren, this state of things should not continue amongst us in this enlightened age, for we believe that it is one of the great means, and well calculated to improve the minds of the youths of our land—to help them to God. We would, therefore, recommend the Churches composing this body, to more strictly adhere and attend to this good Institution, in order that the desired object may be accomplished. All of which is respectfully submitted. B. LANIER, Chairman.

The report of the Committe on the Bible and Publication Society was next received, and is as follows:

Dear Brethren—Your Committee to whom was referred the consideration the North Carolina Baptist Bible and Publication Society, beg leave to report the following: We believe it to be an enterprise worthy of the consideration and support of every Baptist in our Association. We think it is an enterprise well calculated, if properly managed, to send the Bible with its blessings to the houses of many who are destitute of religion and its comforts, to furnish them with religious reading and our own denominational works, which they otherwise would be without. All of which is respectfully submitted. W. C. PATTERSON, Chairman.

The following is the report of the Committee on Education. Several appropriate remarks were made by brethren Jordan, Crutchfield, Weaver, Patterson and Eaton, on the subject. Report received:

Your Committee on Education beg leave to report the following: They would recommend to your body a more thorough system of Education in our denomination, and that Schools of high standing and moral worth be established and patronised, preparatory to Wake Forest College. Your Committee urge the importance of patronising our own Schools and concentrating our efforts in this matter. Let us all remember that we, who are now on the stage of action must soon pass away, and from the rising generation must come our Preachers, Statesmen, Doctors and Lawyers. And how important it is that matters of such weighty import fall into the hands of educated men, that rising generations may enjoy the same liberties and blessings that we of the nineteenth century enjoy. All of which is respectfully submitted.

W. C. PATTERSON, Chairman.

The Committee on State Convention being called on made, the following report :

. The Baptist State Convention of North Carolina, is a general Association of the Baptists of Middle and Eastern North Carolina, formed by delegates from Churches and Associations, for the purpose of concentrating their efforts in carrying out the great command of our Lord, to go and preach the Gospel to every creature. The Convention was formed about twenty-five years ago, and has been instrumental in awakening in some degree our Churches to christian enterprise and benevolence. The objects of the Convention are three. First, the sending of the Gospel into the destitute portions of our own State. Secondly, to assist in sending the Gospel to heathen of other nations. And thirdly, to educate the rising Ministry. The Convention has now no Foreign Board of Missions, the monies appropriated to this object being transmitted directly to the General Board of Foreign Missions, at Richmond, Va. The Domestic Board of the Convention attends to the Home or State Missionaries, and also to the Educational Interest. This Board is located in Milton, N. C., N. J. Palmer, Corresponding Secretary.— The Board has in its employ seven Missionaries, and under its patronage from four to five beneficiaries. The labors of the Missionaries have been greatly blessed. Your committee feel happy in being able to recommend to you an organization so well adapted to the wants of our denomination in this State, and earnestly recommend the co-operation of this Association. Ten dollars is the amount necessary to constitute a delegate for one year. Thirty dollars entitles a brother or sister, when paid at one time, to a life membership. All of which is repectfully submitted.     W. C. PATTERSON, Ch'n.

5. On motion, the Committee appointed on the Friendship Church reported. On motion, report received and Committee discharged :

Your Committee, to whom was referred the case of the New Friendship Church, report that there is a Church consisting of twenty-three members all in peace. Respectfully submitted.     AQUILLA JONES,
JOSEPH SPURGEN,
JONA. WELCH.

6. On motion, agreed to appoint two Missionaries to ride three months in the bounds of this Association, and receive twenty dollars per month each, to be chosen out of the body.

On motion, a Committee of three be appointed to procure

the services of the above missionaries, to wit: James Wiseman, R. Witherington and Jesse Jones.

7. On motion, appointed the ordained Ministers of this Association a standing Presbytery for this year, and three of them to form a quorum.

8. On motion of bro. R. Witherington, agreed that this Association pay the travelling expenses of all delegates appointed from this, and attending sister Associations.

9. Called off till two o'clock.

10. Resumed business. On motion, the Committee on Church Letters and state of Religion reported. Report received and Committee discharged:

The Committee to whom was referred Church Letters and state of Religion within the bounds of this Association, report as follows:

Dear brethren—There has been but few additions to our Churches during the Associational year; consequently we think Religion is in a low state amongst us in general. We would, therefore, recommend as the best means in our judgment for a better state of things amongst us, the holding Camp and other protracted meetings during the ensuing year. All of which is respectfully submitted   WM. OWEN, Ch'n.

11. On motion of bro. James Wiseman, the memorial of the five members of New Friendship Church be laid on the table indefinitely.

12. On motion, bro. A. Williams be exempted from the two dollars lost, and report the balance of the collection taken up on the Sabbath, amounting to $22 37 cents, for Domestic Missions.

13. On motion of bro. Gm. Tussey, that we request bro. Wm. C. Patterson to write out the sermon preached by him on Sabbath, for publication in the Biblical Recorder.

14. On motion, agreed that further time be given to the Committe to secure Missionaries to travel in the bounds of this Association.

15. RESOLVED, That this Association return their thanks to the brethren and friends for their liberality in supporting this meeting during its sessions.

16: We further authorise the Clerk to have 500 copies of the Minutes printed and distribute them as usual.

17. On motion, we adjourn to the time and place of the next session of the body. Singing and prayer by Elder Wm. Turner.

JOSEPH SPURGEN, *Moderator.*

AZARIAH WILLIAMS, *Secretary.*

# TABULAR VIEW OF THE CHURCHES.

| CHURCHES. | COUNTIES. | POST OFFICES. | BY WHOM SUPPLIED. | NAMES OF DELEGATES. | Baptized. | Rec. by Letter. | Restored. | Dis. by Letter. | Excluded. | Deceased. | Whites. | Colored. | Total Number. | Funds. $ cts | Church Meetings. |
|---|---|---|---|---|---|---|---|---|---|---|---|---|---|---|---|
| Lick Creek, | Davidson, | Jackson Hill, | A. Kinney, | M. Redwine, Joseph Kirk, Sampson Newsom, | 3 | 4 | | 1 | | 1 | 85 | 1 | 86 | 1 85 | 48 |
| Jersey, | Do. | Cotton Grove, | A. Weaver, | A. Weaver, James Wiseman, Wm. Owen, | 1 | 1 | | 1 | | 1 | 107 | 1 | 108 | 00 | 1 |
| Abbott's Creek, | Do. | Abbott's Creek, | B. Lanier, | Jesse Jones, A. Jones, Joseph Spurgen, | 1 | 2 | | 2 | | 2 | 139 | | 139 | 2 46 | 3 |
| Tom's Creek, | Do. | Healing Springs, | B. Lanier, | Wm. Yarbrough, P. Riley, Simeon Sheets, | 6 | | | 1 | | | 28 | 4 | 28 | 00 | 3 |
| Jamestown, | Guilford, | Jamestown, | O. Churchill, | James Greenwod, O. Churchill, J. Welch, | | 2 | | 2 | | | 24 | | 32 | 1 00 | 1 |
| Liberty, | Davidson, | Fair Grove, | B. Lanier, | S. S. Lambeth, J. Copple, H. Copple, | 6 | 1 | | 1 | | | 24 | | 24 | 1 34 | 8 |
| Holloway's, | Do. | Silver Hill, | A. Kinney, | J. Huffman. Wm. Newsom, F. Beanblossom | | 1 | | 2 | | 1 | 54 | | 54 | 75 | 2 |
| New Friendship, | Forsythe, | Salem, | Wm. Turner, | A. Delap. J. Styers, J. R. Nichols, | | | | 1 | | 1 | 52 | 29 | 81 | 1 00 | 2 |
| Big Creek, | Montgomery, | Wind Hill, | B. Lanier, | Wm. R. Coggin, Eli Davis, Wm. Hamilton, | 4 | 1 | | 1 | | | 28 | | 81 | 1 00 | 2 |
| Pine M. House, | Davidson, | Lexington, | No supply, | A. Williams, Gm. Tussey, J. A. Cornish, | | | | | | | | | 11 | 1 00 | 2 |
| Reed's X Roads, | Do. | Do. | A. Yarbrough, | R. Witherington. J. Green, R. S. Green, | 1 | 1 | | 1 | | | 47 | 5 | 52 | 00 | 4 |
| Marion, | Do. | Salisbury, | No supply, | Wm. Lambeth, A. G. Allen, | 1 | 1 | | | | | 62 | 1 | 63 | 2 10 | 2 |
| Salisbury, | Rowan, | | | | 1 | | | | | | 17 | | 17 | 60 | 4 |

*A List of Ordained Preachers in this Association.*—A. Kinney, of Lick Creek; B. Lanier, of Tom's Creek; Wm. Turner, of the Jersey; A. Williams, of Reed's Cross Roads; Wm. Lambeth, of Salisbury.

*Licentiates.*—Gm. Tussey; A. Yarbrough, of Reed's Cross Roads; John Teague, of Abbott's Creek, Dempsey Parks; Lick Creek.

# MINUTES

OF THE

## TWENTY THIRD SESSION

OF THE

# LIBERTY BAPTIST ASSOCIATION.

HELD AT

## LICK CREEK MEETING HOUSE.

DAVIDSON COUNTY, N. C.

*August 24, 25, 27, 1855.*

ORIN CHURCHILL, Printer, Greensboro', N. C.

1855.

# PROCEEDINGS

OF

# LIBERTY ASSOCIATION.

LICK CREEK MEETING HOUSE, DAVIDSON  
COUNTY, August 24, 1855.

The members of the Liberty Asssciation met accord,
ing to adjournment, when in the absence of bro. Wm.
Turner, Bro. B. Lanier Preached the Introductory Sermon, from Mathew, 24th, 14.

1. After a short intermission, the members met again-
the Association was called to order by B. Laneir.

2. The Churches were then called to order by bro.
B. Lanier, (acting as Moderator *pro tem*,) when their letters were presented, and their contents noted. (See last
page.)

3. The Delegates present proceeded to the choice of
a Moderator for the present term, which resulted in the
election of brother Benjamin Lanier.

4. On motion no Minister is entitled to vote in the
Association, but the ordained Ministers in the same.

5. On motion appointed breth. Wm. Lambeth, Wm.
Owen, J. Spurgen, A. Kinney, P. Riley, with the Clerk
and Moderator, a Committee to arrange business during
the Association. And I. A. Parks, J. A. Cornish a Committee of Finance.

On motion, appointed breth. A. Kinney, J. Kirk, and
P. Riley, J. Adderton a Committee to arrange preaching
during the Association. Except on Sabbath.

On motion, adjourned until Saturday nine o'clock, A.
M. Prayer by A. Weaver.

*Saturday Morning,* 9 *o'clock.*

Met according to adjournment. Prayer by brother Churchill.

On motion, the Committee of arrangements reported. The report was received and Committee continued.

Invitation to transient Ministers to take seats with us, H. Woodward, presented himself.

2. Called on Correspondents from sister Associations to take seats with us. When breth, J. H. Davis, A. Weaver from the Yadkin, came forward and were welcomed to a seat by the Moderator, and gave the right hand of fellowship. Bro. T. S. Yarbrough, from Sandy Creek, Thomas H. Pritchard, Agent for Wake Forest College, and Wm. M. Faulkner from the Beulah Association, who were cordially received.

3. Called on correspondents from sister Associations to report. Bro. John A. Cornish attended the Yadkin, and was received cordially and had an interesting time.

Bro. Wm. Craver attended the Pedee Association, and was received, those brethren appointed who failed to attend, gave satisfactory excuse.

4. On motion, appointed the following Correspondents to sister Associations. To the Yadkin, breth. Jesse Green, A. R. Witherington and A. Williams, to be held at———on Saturday before the 1st. Sabbath in Oct.

On motion, of brother Wm. Lambeth, we drop correspondence with the Brier Creek Association for the present.

To Sandy Creek, first Sabbath in October, to commence on Friday, to be held with the Antioch Church. Brethren, O. Churchill, A. Kinney, J. Spurgen.

To Pee Dee. To commence on Friday before the fourth Sabbath in September, Brethren Eli Davis, Wm. Hamelton, B. Lanier.

To the Beulah, brethren, Wm. Turner, John Teague, Orin Churchill.

5. On motion, appointed breth. Thos. Yarbro, Wm. Lambeth, I. A. Parks, and A. Williams a Committee to bring out a report on High School.

On motion the following Committees were appointed. On Missions, T. S. Yarbro, A. Williams, and Wm. Owen.

6. On motion, agreed to hold the next annual meeting of this body, with Abbott's Creek Church, near Brown Town, to commence on Friday before the fourth Sabbath in August 1856.

7. On motion, appointed bro. A. Williams, to preach the Introductory sermon, and bro. Lanier, is alternate.

8. On motion, we appoint the Ministers of this Association a Committee to visit the Marion Church, and Pine M. House, and meet on Thursday, after the third Sabbath in September, at Marion to hold a meeting with that Church.

9. Called off until 2 o'clock.

Resumed business again, when E. L. Parker came forward and was received as a Delegate from Pee Dee.

10. On motion, the Committee of Finance, reported that, they had received from the Churches                    $ 15.75.
Funds in the hands of the Treas.                                        1 00.

                                                                                                      16.75.

Report received, Committee discharged.

11. On motion, the Committee on Missions reported, and adopted, and Committee discharged. (See Letter at) when some very appropriate remarks were made by bro. Thomas Yarbro.

12. On motion, of bro. Williams, appointed bro. William Turner as Missionary to Waughtown, and rely on his own sources for support, and report to the next Association.

13. On motion, appointed breth. J. Wiseman, A. Palmer, and Wm. Owen, a Committee, to employ A. Colporteur to labor in this Association entirely under the control of the Committee.

14. The Committee on High School reported, when several appropriate remarks were made by bro. Yarbro, and bro. Pritch

ard the agent of Wake Forest College, and A. Weaver, the report was received and the Committee discharged.

15. On motion, adopted the Resolution offered appointing the Trustees for the High School, at Reed's X Roads, which is as follows,

Resolved. That the following persons be appointed in pursuance of the report of Trustees of High School, to be erected at Reed's X Roads, under patronage of this Association, and Auxilary to the Wake Forest College, and seven of them to form a quorum, (To wit) A. R. Craver, I. A. Park, Gen Tussey, Col. John Myers, Benjamin Myers, Col. Wm. Owen, Rev. A. Williams, James Wiseman, Jacob Kimble, Alfred Hargrave, John Mikle, Esqr. Col. Samuel Hargrave, Alexander Dlap, Henry Smith, Rev. Benjamin Lanier, Col. George Smith, John A. Cornish, Abram Palmer, Eli Davis, Rev. Wm. Turner.

16. Late on Saturday, J. Terrell from the Beulah, appeared as a Delegate, and was received, and E. Parker from Pee Dee.

17. The Association, then Proceeded to the choice of Preachers to occupy the Stand on the Sabbath, which resulted in the choice, of bro. A. Weaver, T. S. Yarbro, Thomas H. Pritchard.

18. On motion, adjourned until Monday morning 9 o'clock, Prayer by T. S. Yarbro.

---

## SABBATH.

The brethren appointed to occupy the Stand, met a large Congregation, when bro. Pritchard, Preached from 2nd Timothy, 11 v. "According to the glorious Gospel of Jesus Christ."

At 10 o'clock, T. S. Yarbro, from Mat. 6th, 10 v. "Thy Kingdom come."

At 3 o'clock, P M A. Weaver, from Daniel 2nd. 44th v. The word preached seemed satisfactory, and made deep impressions on the hearers.

---

MONDAY MORNING, 9 o'clock, *August the 27th*, 1855.

Met according to adjournment, Prayer by bro T. S. Yarbro.

1. On motion, of bro. Wm. Lambeth, appointed all the Ordained Ministers of this Association a Standing Presbytery during life, on their good behavior, and three of them to form a quorum.

2. For the present, we pass over holding the meeting of the Bible & Publication Society, for the present year.

3. On motion, the Committee of arrangements reported, and Committee discharged.

4. On motion, appointed breth. John A. Cornish, S M. Charles, and in case of failure, A. Weaver, Delegates to the Baptist State Convention, held at Warrenton in November.

The Public collection taken up on Sabbath amounting to $14.50 cts. and the collection taken up on monday in the Association, amounting to $ 7.50, making in all $ 22.50, it was paid over to bro. T. S. Yarbro for the use of the Convention.

5. On motion, we empower the Committee to employ a Missionary to ride in this Association, in connection with a Colporteur, to rely on their field for support.

6. Resolved. That the Association return their thanks to the brethren and friends, for their liberality in supporting this meeting during its Session.

7. We further authorise the Clerk to have 500 copies of the Minutes printed and distribute them as usual.

8. On motion, we adjourn to the time and place of the next Session of the Body. Singing and prayer by bro. Lambeth.

B. LANIER, Moderator.

AZARIAH WILLIAMS Clerk.

Immediately after adjournment, the Presbytery proceeded to the Ordination of Brother Orin Churchill, after a satisfactory Examination in the following manner, (to wit)

Brother B. Lanier, the Ordination Prayer. Wm. Lambeth, extended the Bible. A. Williams, gave the Charge. A. Kinney the right hand of fellowship.

------------

## Report on Missions.

Your Committee are sorry to learn that so little has been done in Missionary labor during the past year among us.

The spread of the gospel, is doubtless the great work of the Church of Jesus Christ. In this glorious work every christian should engage with zeal, and at the same time, with prudence and foresight.

We hope that this Association, will devise some plan by which every Church at least shall be supplied with monthly preaching.

A Licensed minister sent out as a Missionary Colporteur, to carry books, and spread from house to house, we think might do much good. Where a Church cannot sustain their ministery, we would recommend that the Association request ministers to visit it alternately, and supply it with the preached word. In such cases, the stronger Churches we recommend to send up to the Association their contributions to remunerate these brethren for their service.

We recommend the appointment of bro. Wm. Turner as Missionary to Waughtown, to preach there once a month or oftener.

WM. OWEN, Chairman.

## REPORT OF THE COMMITTEE ON HIGH SCHOOL.

Your Committee learn with pleasure, that the brethren and friends in the neighborhood of Reed's ⋈ Roads, are desirous of building a High School in that vicinity, and wish this body to extend to it, its patronage and encouragement. Your Committee would therefore recommend that the Association proceed to appoint a board of Trustees for the School, and hereafter fill all vacancies that may occur. Let every Baptist and friend of Education, do something for this School, both by subscription and patronage.

# TABULAR VIEW OF THE CHURCHES.

| CHURCHES. | COUNTIES. | POST OFFICES. | BY WHOM SUPPLIED | DELEGATES NAMES. | Baptized. | Rec'd by Letter. | Restored. | Dis. by Letter. | Excluded. | Deceased. | White. | Colored. | Total number. | Funds {cts. | Ch. Meetings. |
|---|---|---|---|---|---|---|---|---|---|---|---|---|---|---|---|
| Lick Creek, | Davidson, | Jacks Hill, | A Kinney, | A Kinney, J Adderton, J Kirk, | 2 | | | 3 | 1 | 1 | 83 | 1 | 84 | 1.90 | 1 |
| Jersey, | Do. | Union Grove, | A Weaver, | Wm Owen H Smith J Wiseman | 5.00 | | | 1.00 | 7 | | 105 | 133 | 238 | 1.90 | 17 |
| Abbott's Creek, | Do. | Abbott's Creek, | Wm Turner, | Wm Clinard J Spurgen J Jones | 8 | | | 1.00 | 1 | 2 | 91 | 2 | 93 | 2.00 | 2 |
| Tom's Creek. | Do. | Healing Springs, | B Lanier, | P Riley, J Shepperd, S Saeets | | | | 1.00 | 1 | 4 | 28 | 4 | 32 | 1.00 | 2 |
| Jamestown, | Guilford, | Jamestown, | O Churchill, | O Churchill J Welsh, B Harris | 1.00 | | | 1.00 | 1 | | 23 | | 23 | 1.00 | 4 |
| Liberty, | Davidson | Fair Grove, | H Copple, | H Copple, B May, L Garret, | | 1 | | | 4.00 | | 46 | | 50 | 1.00 | 4 |
| Holloway's, | Do. | Silver Hill, | A Palmer, | A Palmer, G Cross, Jno. Cross, | | | | | | | 49 | 1 | 50 | 1.00 | 4 |
| New Friendsh' | Forsvihe, | Naughtown, | Wm Turner, | Delap J Charles S M Charles | | | | 5.00 | | | 46 | 29 | 75 | 1.00 | 2 |
| Big Creek, | Montgomery, | Wird Hill, | B Lanier, | Eli Davis W Hamel' W Crowder | 6 | | | | | | 36 | | 36 | 1.00 | 2 |
| Pine M. House | Davidson, | Lexington, | No supply, | | 1.00 | | | 2.00 | | | 46 | | 57 | 1.00 | 2 |
| Reel's X Roads | Do. | " | A Weaver, | J A Cornish A Parks A Wood | | | | | | | 10 | | 10 | | |
| Marion, | Do. | " | A Weaver, | R S Green, R Witherington, | 6.00 | | | | 1 | | 1 | 3 | 71 | 1.50 | 2 |
| Salisbury, | Rowan, | Salisbury, | No supply, | Wm Lambeth, | 1.00 | | | | | | 18 | 3 | 21 | | 4 |
| | | | | | 35 | 5 | 1 | 12 | 8 | 16 | 620 | 173 | 847 | 15 75 | 1 |

A LIST OF ORDAINED PREACHERS IN THIS ASSOCIATION.—A. Kinney, of Lick Creek; B. Lanier, of Tom's Creek; Wm. Turner, of the Jersey; A. Williams, of Reed's Cross Roads; Wm. Lambeth, of Salisbury; Orin Churchill, of James Town.

LICENTIATES.—Gin. Tussey, A. Yarbrough, of Reed's Cross Roads; Dempsey Parks, Lick Creek.

# MINUTES

OF THE

## TWENTY FOURTH SESSION

OF THE

## Liberty Baptist Association,

HELD AT

Abbotts Creek M. H., near Brown Town, Davidson County, N. C.

## AUGUST 22, 23, 25, 1856.

PUBLISHED BY ORDER OF THE ASSOCIATION.

LEXINGTON, N. C.
LEXINGTON AND YADKIN FLAG PRESS.
1856.

# Proceedings of Liberty Association.

The members of Liberty Association, met according to adjournment. The introductory Sermon was preached by Bro. A. Williams, from Ro. 10—1.

1. After a short intermission, the members met again. The Association was called to order by our former Moderator. Letters handed in—contents noted. See last p.

2. The Delegates present, proceeded to the choice of Moderator for the present term, which resulted in the choice of Bro. B. Lanier.

3. On petition, the Church at Greensborough was received by the Moderator, giving right hand of fellowship as a member of this body. (See last page.)

4. Called on correspondents from Sister Associations to take seats with us; when Bro. J. McDaniel, from the Sandy Creek came forward, and Bro. Herriford, the Beulah, and was cordially received by the Moderator, giving right hand of fellowship. Also, Bro. D. Wright, from Pedee, and was received cordially.

5. On motion, appointed Bro. A. Weaver, Wm. Turner, Wm. Lambeth, with the Moderator and Clerk, a Committee of Arrangements.

6. Bro. J. C. Averitt and Bro. O. Churchill, a Committee of Finance.

On motion, adjourned until to-morrow 9 o'clock, A. M. Prayer by Bro. A. Weaver.

SATURDAY, AUGUST 29.

Met according to previous adjournment. Religious services by Bro. Wm. Turner.

On motion, Committee of Arrangements reported. The report recived and Committee continued.

1. Appoint the following Committees on Church letters and state of religion. Bro. Wm. Turner, Bro. Isaac Kinney and S. Newsom. On Sabbath Schools, Bro. A. Weaver, Wm. R. Coggin and B. May. On Missions, Bro. J. C. Averitt, Wm. S. Herriford and J. A Parks. On Bible and Publication Society, Bro. James McDaniel, Aquilla Jones and Wm. Lambeth. On the Baptist State Convention, Bro. A. Williams, A. Weaver and B. G. Charles. On motion of Bro. A. Weaver, the document from Nashville was received; read and referred to the Committee on Bible and Publication.

2. Invitation given to transient Ministers, with licentiates to take seats with us. Bro. J. A. Cornish, came forward, and was recived.

3. On motion, the Committe on Finance, reported: Report received, Committee discharged.

4. Call on Correspondents to Sister Associations to report. All the Brethren that failed to attend, were excused, but requested to attend punctually for the future.

5. Appointed Correspondents to the following Associations, to the Yadkin, to be held with Cross Road Church, Davie County, Bro. Wm. Lambeth, Wm. Turner and A. Williams, on Saturday before the first Sabbath in October. To Sandy Creek, Bro. A. Weaver, B. Lanier and O. Churchill to be held at Mays Chapel, eight miles South of Pittsborough, to commence Friday, before the first Sabbath in October.

To the Pedee, to commence on Friday before the Second Sabbath in October, Bro. B. Lanier, John Redwine and A. Palmer. To be held at Spring Hill, to Buelah brethren; A. Weaver, Wm. Turner and John Teague, to commence on Friday before the 3d Sabbath in Aug. 1857.

6. On motion, the report of the Committee on Missions and Colportage, was received (see letter A.) and discharged.

7. Called on Missionaries to report, when Bro. A. Weaver, reported. (See appendix B.)

Bro. Wm. Turner, Missionary to Waughtown, reported. (See Letter C.)

On motion, took a recess of one hour. Benediction by the Moderator.

Met pursuant to adjournment.

8. On motion, agreed to have a missionary for the ensueing year, and proceeded to the choice of one, which terminated in choosing Bro. A. Weaver.

9. On motion, agreed to appoint a board on Missions, consisting of a member from each Church, and five of them to form a quorum, when the following Brethren were appointed. To wit—Wm. R. Coggin, Wm. Owen, Aquilla Jones, John Skeen, Jonathan Welch, Henry Copple, A. Palmer, A. Delap, Enoch Davis, J. A. Parks, Wm. Lambeth, Benjamin Churchill and R. S. Green, to hold their meetings, the fifth Sunday in every month that has five Sundays, with the Saturday before, at Lexington, to transact business.

10. On motion, agreed to hold the next annual meeting of this body, with Reeds Cross Roads Church, five miles west of Lexington, to commence on Friday before the fourth Sabbath, in August 1857.

11. On motion, appointed Bro. Wm. Turner, to preach the Introductory Sermon, and Bro. Wm. Lambeth, his alternate.

On motion, this Association request Bro. Turner, to preach a doctrinal discourse, choosing his subject.

12. On motion, the Association proceeded to the choice of Preachers to occupy the stand on the Sabbath, which resulted in the choice of Bro. James McDaniel, A. Weaver and Wm. Turner, and Bro. James McDaniel to preach a Missionary Sermon at 11 o'clock. A. M.—take up a collection for domestic mission in our midst.

13. On motion, adjourned until Monday morning at 9 o'clock. Prayer by Elder Wm. Lambeth.

SABBATH.

The Ministers appointed to preach on this day, met a large, respectable and orderly congregation, at 9 o'clock, Bro. Wm. Turner, preached from Joel the 2 chapter 13 verse. Bro. James McDaniel, of Fayetteville, followed from Zachriah 13 chapter 1st, verse. A collection, was then taken up amounting to $11,63 for the use of domestic missions, after a recess of one hour, or at 3 o'clock P. M. Bro. A. Weaver, preached from 2nd Kings, 5th chapter 12th verse, all of which was very interesting and satisfactory.

MONDAY MORNING, AUGUST 25th.

The Association met according to previous adjournment, and after prayer by Elder Amos Weaver, the Association proceeded to business in the following manner:

1. On motion, Bro. A. Weaver, reported on Sabbath Schools. (See letter D.) Report received and Committee discharged.

Committee on Church letters and state of Religion, reported. Report adopted and Committee discharged. (E)

On missions, reported. Report received and Committee discharged. (F)

On Bible and Publication Society, reported. (See G) Report adopted, Committee discharged, and also adopted the resolution.

On motion, agreed to give Bro. Williams time to write a report at home, on the Baptist State Convention, and confer with Bro. A. Weaver, one of the Committee, and attach the report to the Ministers.

2. On motion, the Association proceeded to the organization of a Bible and Publication Society, when they proproceed to elect their officers. See further proceedings.

3. On motion, appointed Bro. Wm. Turner, Missionary in the northern portion of this Association, relying on his field for support.

Also, on motion, appointed Bro. Wm. Lambeth, Missionary in Rowan County, relying on his field for support, and Bro. A. Williams, to the Piney Meeting House.

4. On motion, proceeded to elect Bro. Wm. Turner, to preach the Missionary sermon, on Sabbath, at our next annual meeting, at 11 o'clock, A. M.

On motion, the Clerk is directed to write to the board of the Convention, requesting them to appoint A. Weaver, riding Missionary in the bounds of this Association.

And we appoint Bro. John C. Averitt, delegate to the Baptist State Convention.

5. On motion, the delegates proceeded to pledge for the Churches or individuals, the sum announced to their names, to raise a fund to pay our Missionary for the ensueing year, which is a part of his salary.

| | |
|---|---|
| Bro. William Coggin, for Lick Creek, | $10 00 |
| Isaac Kinney, E. Merrill, for Jersey, | 10.00 |
| Aquilla Jones, Abbotts Creek, | 10.00 |
| For himself, | 5.00 |
| S. Newsom, do., Toms Creek, | 7.50 |
| Jonathan Welsh, do., James Town, | 6.00 |
| Benjamin May, do., Liberty, | 6.00 |
| Abram Palmer, do., Holloway's, | 5.00 |
| S. M. Charles, do., New Friendship, | 5.00 |
| Eli Coggin, do., Big Creek, | 5.00 |
| I. A. Parks, for self or Church at Reed's Cross Roads... | 5.00 |
| Benjamin Churchill, for Greensborough, | 5.02 |
| | $83.50 |

6. *Resolved,* That the Association return their thanks to the brethren and friends for their liberality in supporting this Meeting during its Session.

7. We further authorize the Clerk to have 500 copies of the Minutes printed, and distribute them as usual.

8. On motion, we adjourn to the time and place of the next Session of this Body, when a few touching and appropriate remarks were made by elder John C. Averitt, and concluded with singing and prayer.

BENJAMIN LANIER, Moderator.

AZARIAH WILLIAMS, Clerk.

## CONSTITUTION OF AN ASSOCIATIONAL BIBLE SOCIETY.

In order that we may more systematically and effectually co-operate with the Baptist Bible Society of this State and the Bible Board of the Southern Baptist Convention, in the great work of circulating the Holy Scriptures in our own and other lands, we hereby form ourselves into a Bible Society to act in connexion with this Association, and adopt the following Constitution.

# CONSTITUTION.

ARTICLE I. This Society shall be called the Bible Society of the Liberty Association.

### OF MEMBERS.

ARTICLE II. This Society shall be composed of the following classes of persons:

1st. Of all the messengers sent up with funds from congregational or other local bible societies, which shall be entitled to one delegate for every five dollars sent up.

2nd. Of representatives of Churches, Missionary Societies, Sunday Schools, or any other bodies which shall send up funds, one delegate for every five dollars sent up.

3d. Of all persons who shall have paid five dollars or more, at any one time to this Society, or to any of its auxiliaries. Such persons shall be counted members for life.

4th. Of all persons who are present at any meeting of the Society and contribute the sum of fifty cents shall be considered members for the year.

ARTICLE III. The object of this Society shall be to aid in circulation of the Holy Scriptures in our own and other lands; and the funds collected by us shall be sent up to the State Baptist Bible Society of our own State, or to the Bible Board of the Southern Baptist Convention at Nashville.

### OF OFFICERS.

ARTICLE IV. The Officers of this Society shall be a President, three Vice Presidents, a Secretary and Treasurer, who shall perform the duties common to officers in similar organizations; and shall be elected by a plurality of votes at each annual meeting; and in case of a failure to elect, shall hold their places until another meeting.

## OF MEETINGS.

ARTICLE V. The regular annual meetings of this Society shall be held at the same time and place with the meetings of our Association, at which the following order of business shall be observed:

1st. The reports of the Treasurer and of the Board of Directors shall be read.

2d. A sermon, or other addresses suitable to the occasion, shall be delivered.

3d. An opportunity given to those present to become members, by subscribing or contributing to our funds, and a general collection taken up.

4th. Officers elected and speakers appointed for the next meeting. An adjourned meeting may be held at any time, or one may be called at any time, by the President or either of the Vice Presidents.

## OF LIFE DIRECTORS.

ARTICLE VI. Any person who shall contribute to our funds the sum of twenty dollars, at any one time, or in two annual installments, shall be considered life directors, and with the officers of the Society, shall constitute a Board to attend to any business in the interests of the regular meetings.

ARTICLE VII. This Constitution may be altered or amended by a vote of two thirds of the members present at any regular meeting.

The Bible Society, after their organization proceeded to elect officers for the present year, which resulted as follows: A. Williams, President; Isaac Kinney, first Vice President; J.A. Parks, second Vice President; Wm. Turner, third Vice President; John C. Averitt, Secretary and Treasurer.

## LIFE MEMBERS.

A. Williams, J. A. Parks, Alexander Delap, Isaac Kinney, Benjamin Lanier.

## ANNUAL MEMBERS BY THE PAYMENT OF FIFTY CENTS.

J. C. Averitt, Aquilla Jones, John Teague, William Turner, John Redwine, John Charles, Aquilla Teague, A. O. P. Teague, Benjamin Churchill, Jonathan Welch.

Amount subscribed,..................................$30.00
Cash received,...................................... 15.50
$14.50

Elder John C. Averitt, was apointed to deliver an address before the B. B. Society at our next annual Association.   A. WILLIAMS, PRESIDENT.

JOHN C. AVERITT, SECRETARY.

---

### REPORT OF COMMITTEE ON FINANCE.

Received from the Churches.....................$17,72½
Funds in the hand of the Treasurer................. 1.50
Total on hand at the present....................$19.22½

(A.)

*The Committee appointed at last Association on Home Missions and Colportage, beg leave to report—*

That they found some difficulty in geting a Minister to travel in the bounds of the Association; generally with no certain compensation. However, we engaged Elder Amos Weaver some time the past Spring to devote a portion of his time as Missionary and Colporteur within the bounds of our Association, to rely entirely on his field for his support. All of which is respectfully submitted; by...

ABRAM PALMER, CHAIRMAN.

(B.)

### MISSIONARY'S REPORT.

I have, since my selection by your Committee as Missionary and Colportuer for this Association, not been able to obtain books, and as such have done nothing in the way of Colportage.

I have spent, in preaching and travelling, some twelve to fifteen days; which, together with time set apart, for the same purpose, but which was not required, owing to meeting not being continued as long as anticipated. Worked some two thirds of a month.

I have received from the Churches the following amounts, to wit:

From Hollowell's,............................ $3.50
   "   Lick Creek,.......................... 6.75
   "   Big Creek,........................... 6.90
   '.   Liberty,.............................. 3.75

All of which is respectfully submitted, by

AMOS WEAVER, Missionary.

(c.)

*The following Report submitted by William Turner,— Missionary at Waughtown—*

I have preached thirteen sermons, baptised five of that congregation, and received Ten dollars and sixty three cents compensation.

(d.)

## REPORT ON SABBATH SCHOOLS.

*The Committee on Sabbath Schools, beg leave to submit the following Report—*

In looking over the field, of our operation, and surveying the numerous instrumentalities now within the Church of Christ, your Committee are of the deliberate opinion that few—if any—of the legitimate labours to which the Church is invited, are so full of hope, or promise so rich and so gracious a return as Sabbath Schools. Yet, your Committee, with regret, have to state that this inviting field lies with us almost wholy uncultivated. It was a circumstance regarded by St. Paul as exceedingly auspicious in the life of an imminent son of his in the Gospel, " That from a child, he had known the Holy Scriptures," and there is no means known to your Committee equal to a well conducted Sabbath School to familiarize the young mind with the word of God.

Solomon says, "Train up a child in the way he should go, and when he is old, he will not depart therefrom." It will be said, perhaps, that parental training is here alluded to. Be it so. Still, it is a most appalling truth, that pious parental training is far from being general. Perhaps, in few cases is this so perfectly attained to in the family, as to render the Sabbath School unnecessary; while, in very many instances, the children and youth of our country must and will continue to grow up in the most deplorable ignorance and vice; and, consequently, become the pest of both, Church and State, who might, under proper moral culture, seasonably and judiciously applied, become ornaments to both. This defect in parental training can only be met by the Church, through the agency of the Sabbath School. And none can doubt that it is the legitimate and sacred duty of the Church to look after this thing. And even under the most favourable circumstances, it has been found that Sabbath Schools are of invaluable advantage in strengthening and in forming parental religious cultivation.

Again, it is believed that among the happy results that usually attend the labours of a well conducted Sabbath School, the reflex influence on those teachers and superintendants engaged in conducting them, is by no means the least of their results. In the whole range of divine obligation, God has graciously blended our duty with our instincts; and this principle is not less positive and operative in the matter under consideration. Those who engaged for any considerable length of time, heartily, in the delightful task of impressing the minds of our children and youth, with the duties of religion and obligations o f piety, cannot fail to have the sphere of their own knowledge of God—His law and government enlarged—their hearts enobled, and their Spiritual graces improved.— Thus, Sabbath Schools are in a two fold sense the nurseries of the Church—aiding and enforcing on the one hand parental efforts; and on the other, rendering powerful and effective, the living ministry, when it must, without them, be faintiless and inoperative. Your Committee, in view of the above facts and considerations, beg leave to offer the following Resolution and recommend its adoption: "Resolved, That this Association recommend each Church within our bounds to form Sabbath Schools at their respective Meeting Houses, or at such other place or places, as they shall find most convenient, that they take such steps in regard to the same as to have their Schools regular organizations, and that they send up their Delegates to the next Association, with full return of their proceedings on this matter with authority to organize, during that meeting of our Body, an Associational Sabbath School Society, to which each, in our bounds, may act as auxiliary.

All of which is respectfully submitted.

AMOS WEAVER, CHAIRMAN.

(E.)

*The Committee on Church Letters and state of Religion Report—*

That from the statistics of the Churches in this Association, we find that during the past year, there has been little or no increase. Religion, then, must be in rather a low state. We are taught that when Zion travails, she brings forth: and it is manifest, from the experience of every one, that when the Church is in a luke-warm condition, that there is but little interest felt by the world in matters of religion. If the light of the Christian grows dim in the same proportion, darkness will pervade the earth, and sinners will press onward in the road to ruin; for he that walketh in darkness, knoweth not whither he goeth. There is great responsibility resting upon us. We would say—first to the Ministry: "Cry aloud, spare not; lift thy voice like a trumpet, and show my people their transgressions, and the house of Jacob their sins." And secondly, to the laity, we say: Hold up your Ministers' hands; let them feel, like a mighty engine, the power of your co-operation; and then you will see Zion prospering —for God works through his people; and the religion of Jesus Christ, prompts us to act in this great Scheme of benevolence; and we know that our labour is not in vain with the Lord. The stone cut out without hands became a great Nation and filled the whole earth.

All of which is respectfully submitted.

WILLIAM TURNER, CHAIRMAN.

(F.)

## REPORT ON MISSIONS.

The importance of Missions must be evident to those who are acquainted with the moral condition of the world. The majority of the inhabitants of the globe are still enveloped in Pagan darknes. The glad tidings of salvation through the mediation of Christ has never saluted their ears. It is not necessary, however, to look beyond our own bounds to see the importance of Missions. Even within the limits of Liberty Association, there are many sections almost entirely destitute of preaching of any kind and many other sections destitute of Baptist preaching.— It is to be feared that the Baptists, generally, have not viewed their obligations to disseminate divine truth in the proper light. If a field is occupied by some Protestant denomination, it is not regarded as Missionary ground.— This is a great mistake. Jesus Christ never planted but one Church in the world, and that was composed of immersed believers. To that Church he gave the commission: "Go ye, therefore, into all the world, and preach the Gospel to every creature." Upon this Church the obligation still rests to carry out this commission to its full extent. It is therefore not only our duty to send a Missionary to those places where there is no preaching, but it is also our duty to send a Missionary to those places where the ordinances are not kept as they were delivered by inspired Apostles, a man who is able and willing to defend the distinctive views of the Baptists; and to refute and expose 'peda-Baptist errors. If this course had been

pursued faithfully, in time past, our views would have
been generally known, and would have prevailed to a far
greater extent.   We have insisted chiefly on Missions
within our bounds,, not with a view to under value the
vast importance of Foreign Missions, but because we think
that very little will be done for them unless the Home
Missions are faithfully and successfully prosecuted.  The
most successful way to awaken an interest for Foreign
Missions,—is to arouse the attention of our Churches
to the importance of supplying their own destitution.—
Having appointed a Missionary within our own limits, let
us determine to sustain him by our prayers and our contributions.  Brethren, let us endeavor to labour more and
pray more for the advancement of the Redeemer's Kingdom; let us adopt the prayer of the dying Psalmist :—
" Let the whole earth be filled with His glory.   Amen,
and Amen."   Respectfully submitted.

JOHN C. AVERITT, Chairman.

(G.)
## REPORT ON BAPTIST CONVENTION.

*Your Committee, to whom was refered the subject of the
Convention, submit the following :*

The Convention was organized upwards of twenty-one
years ago, by brethren, whose hearts yearned over dying
men more than over this worlds goods.   Whose chief object was then, and still is, of sending the Gospel to the
destitute portions of our State, and to aid poor young
preachers to obtain an education, to qualify them for the
work of the Ministry—and send the Missionary to the
land of Heathenism, with the blessed Gospel of the Son of
God.

1. When we take a retrospective view of the moral
darkness that still pervades our land, and the great destitution that pervades our Villages, Towns and Neighborhoods, for the bread of life, can we withhold any longer
from aiding the Convention, in sending the Missionary

among those famishing Millions, whose cries are rising up before the Lord of Sabbaoth.

2. And when we leave our own beloved Country, and take a view of those idoldetrous nations, the heart sickens at the awful scenes that transpire. The Mother offering her tender offsprings to Idols, the wife bound to the Funeral pile of her husband, the infirm buried alive, the worshiping of gnats &c., &c., How can any withhold? Who has tested that the Lord is good, from aiding the Convention, in sending the Missionary, among them. Brethren, it requires more than a few empty wishes to accomplish the great work. How much owest thou the Lord? pay thy dues, as it will profit little to say be ye warmed, filled clothed, while ye withhold, the needful things.

3. The Convention has a great and glorious work to accomplish, and no agent in the field this year, but entirely depending on the Liberality of the brethren and friends for help. The Convention has not near enough Missionaries employed to supply the domestic mission, besides they need funds to sustain the beneficiaries already at Wake Forest. To sustain these, it requirers all the means at their command. While many men ought and desire to be there, they nor the Convention, have not the means, and hence the number is small, much has been done, but more remains to be done.

4. The education of the rising Ministry, is a subject of vital importance to the Church. Every other profession is crowded with educated men, and the ministry ought to keep pace with them, in order to instruct, and meet the evils of the infidel and deist. Now brethren permit us to solicit your prayers and alms, in behalf of the Convention, as North Carolina contains at this time, fifty thousand three hundred and twenty three Baptist, according to the last accounts. When we see how little is contributed according to membership, how can we say that we desire the salvation of our fellow being? and make so little or no sacrifice to accomplish it. Let every Baptist do like the

poor widow. in part, throw in their mite into the treasure of the Lord, don't wait for an agent to dun you, but send it up immediately to the Convention, and let those that refuse, ask themselves, have I done what I could, if so, well done thou good and faithful servant.

All of which is respectfully submitted.

ASARIAH WILLIAMS, Chairman.

(h.)

*The Committee to whom was submitted the Bible cause, present the following report—*

The conversion of the world, is obviously the great object for united christian effort. Among the means by which this object is to be attained, the circulation of the Bible, in the various languages of the people, is the most important. By God's Truth, men are to be reformed and converted. The entrance of this word giveth light.— "Sanctify them through thy Truth, thy word is Truth."

The circulation of the Bible is a work committed by God, to the Church. "Ye are the light of the world," so says the Saviour. They are not only to be lights in their character, exhibiting in their temper, spirit, disposition, and manner of living, the excellence of religion ; but they are, by christian effort, to circulate the Bible, this light which shines in a dark place, able to make men wise unto salvation. They are to hold forth the word of life to the nations of the earth, in this way.

The wants that exist for the Bible, in our own country, and in foreign lands, have been made known to this Association by the circular of the Southern Bible Board, which was read on Saturday. God, in his providence, has opened most of the countries to the circulation of the Bible, and a voice seems to call the church to go up and possess the land thus spread out before them.

Your Committee believe this Association to be capable of performing an important part, in this department of christian duty. And they hope that some systematic plan of operation, in aid of this cause, will be adopted at this session, convinced as they are, that the time for action has fully come. They beg leave to present, therefore, the following resolution for the consideration of the Association.

*Resolved*, That this Association organize an Associational Bible Society, to aid in the circulation of the Scriptures.

All of which is respectfully submitted.

JAMES McDANIEL, Chairman.

---

## LIST OF ORDAINED PREACHERS BELONGING TO THIS ASSOCIATION.

Alfred Kinney, of Lick Creek; Benjamin Lanier, of Tom's Creek; Amos Weaver, of Jersey; A. Williams, of Reed's Cross Roads; William Turner, of New Friendship; William Lambeth, and John C. Averitt, of Salisbury; Orin Churchill, of James Town.

Licentiates.—Green Tussey, Aaron Yarborough and John A. Cornish, of Reed's Cross Roads; William R. Coggin and John Redwine, of Lick Creek.

| ates' Names. | BAPTISED. | REC'D BY LETTER. | RESTORED. | DIS BY LETTER. | EXCLUDED. | DECEASED. | WHITE. | COLORED. | TOTAL. | FUNDS $ cts. | CH MEMBERS. |
|---|---|---|---|---|---|---|---|---|---|---|---|
| R. Coggin. John Redwine, | | | | | | 2 | 81 | | 81 | 1 90 | 48 |
| mny, Ebenezer Merrill, | 18 | 2 | | | | 9 | 108 | 145 | 252 | 3 00 | 1 |
| 1 Clinard John Teague, | | 1 | 1 | | | 1 | 91 | 2 | 93 | 3 00 | 3 |
| eets, Sampson Newsom, | 4 | | 3 | | | | 26 | 4 | 30 | 1 00 | 3 |
| Johnson, B Harris, | | | | | | | 24 | | 24 | 1 00 | 4 |
| mbeth, K Miller, | 5 | | 3 | 3 | | 2 | 48 | 1 | 49 | 75 | 38 |
| uth, F. Beanblossom, | 4 | 3 | | | | 1 | 45 | 28 | 73 | 1 00 | 2 |
| Styres, R Y Charles, | | | | | | 1 | 44 | | 44 | 1 50 | 2 |
| Coggin, Ira Hambleton, | 7 | 2 | | 2 | 1 | 2 | 44 | | 44 | 1 50 | 2 |
| Brot'er A Williams, | 4 | 2 | 2 | 2 | | 2 | 46 | 4 | 50 | 1 00 | 3 |
| I. Owen, I A. Park, | 1 | | | | | 1 | 8 | 2 | 10 | 87½ | 48 |
| b, J. C. Averitt, | 2 | 1 | | 5 | | 1 | 69 | 3 | 72 | 50 | 28 |
| John Ingold, Benj. Churchill, | 3 | 3 | 1 | | | 1 | 15 | | 15 | 1 20 | 38 |
| | 3 | 1 | | | | | 44 | | 44 | 55 | |
| | | | | | | | 32 | | 32 | 1 00 | 1 |
| | 44 | 9 | 3 | 19 | 4 | 21 | 681 | 299 | 980 | 17 72½ | |

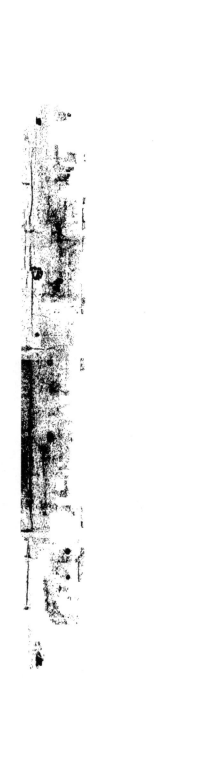

# MINUTES

OF THE

## TWENTY FOURTH SESSION

OF THE

# 𝕷𝖎𝖇𝖊𝖗𝖙𝖞 𝕭𝖆𝖕𝖙𝖎𝖘𝖙 𝕬𝖘𝖘𝖔𝖈𝖎𝖆𝖙𝖎𝖔𝖓,

HELD AT

Abbotts Creek M. H., near Brown Town, Davidson County, N. C.

**AUGUST 22, 23, 25, 1856.**

---

## PUBLISHED BY ORDER OF THE ASSOCIATION.

---

LEXINGTON, N. C.

LEXINGTON AND YADKIN FLAG PRESS.

1856.

# Proceedings of Liberty Association.

ABBOTTS CREEK, M. H., DAVIDSON Co.

FRIDAY, AUGUST 22, 1856.

The members of Liberty Association, met according to adjournment. The introductory Sermon was preached by Bro. A. Williams, from Ro. 10—1.

1. After a short intermission, the members met again. The Association was called to order by our former Moderator. Letters handed in—contents noted. See last p.

2. The Delegates present, proceeded to the choice of Moderator for the present term, which resulted in the choice of Bro. B. Lanier.

3. On petition, the Church at Greensborough was received by the Moderator, giving right hand of fellowship as a member of this body. (See last page.)

4. Called on correspondents from Sister Associations to take seats with us; when Bro. J. McDaniel, from the Sandy Creek came forward, and Bro. Herriford, the Buelah; and was cordially received by the Moderator, giving right hand of fellowship. Also, Bro. D. Wright, from Pedee, and was received cordially,

5. On motion, appointed Bro. A. Weaver, Wm. Turner, Wm. Lambeth, with the Moderator and Clerk, a Committee of Arrangements.

6. Bro. J. C. Averitt and Bro. O. Churchill, a Committee of Finance.

On motion, adjourned until to-morrow 9 o'clock, A. M. Prayer by Bro. A. Weaver.

SATURDAY, AUGUST 29.

Met according to previous adjournment. Religious services by Bro. Wm. Turner.

On motion, Committee of Arrangements reported. The report recived and Committee continued.

1. Appoint the following Committees on Church letters and state of religion. Bro. Wm.Turner, Bro. Isaac Kinney and S. Newsom. On Sabbath Schools, Bro. A. Weaver, Wm. R. Coggin and B. May. On Missions, Bro. J. C. Averitt, Wm. S. Herriford and J. A Parks. On Bible and Publication Society, Bro. James McDaniel, Aquilla Jones and Wm. Lambeth. On the Baptist State Convention, Bro. A. Williams, A. Weaver and B. G. Charles. On motion of Bro. A. Weaver, the document from Nashville was received, read and referred to the Committee on Bible and Publication.

2. Invitation given to transient Ministers, with licentiates to take seates with us. Bro. J. A. Cornish, came forward, and was recived.

3. On motion, the Committe on Finance, reported. Report received, Committee discharged.

4. Call on Correspondents to Sister Associations to report. All the Brethren that failed to attend, were excused, but requested to attend punctually for the future.

5. Appointed Correspondents to the following Associations, to the Yadkin, to be held with Cross Road Church, Davie County, Bro. Wm. Lambeth, Wm. Turner and A. Williams, on Saturday before the first Sabbath in October. To Sandy Creek, Bro. A. Weaver, B. Lanier and O. Churchill to be held at Mays Chapel, eight miles South of Pittsborough, to commence Friday before the first Sabbath in October.

To the Pedee, to commence on Friday before the Second Sabbath in October, Bro. B. Lanier, John Redwine and A. Palmer. To be held at Spring Hill, to Buelah brethren; A. Weaver, Wm. Turner and John Teague, to commence on Friday before the 3d Sabbath in Aug. 1857.

6. On motion, the report of the Committee on Missions and Colportage, was received (see letter A.) and discharged.

7. Called on Missionaries to report, when Bro. A. Weaver, reported. (See appendix B.)

Bro. Wm. Turner, Missionary to Waughtown, reported. (See Letter C.)

On motion, took a recess of one hour. Benediction by the Moderator.

Met pursuant to adjournment.

8. On motion, agreed to have a missionary for the ensueing year, and proceeded to the choice of one, which terminated in choosing Bro. A. Weaver.

9. On motion, agreed to appoint a board on Missions, consisting of a member from each Church, and five of them to form a quorum, when the following Brethren were appointed. To wit—Wm. R. Coggin, Wm. Owen, Aquilla Jones, John Skeen, Jonathan Welch, Henry Copple, A. Palmer, A. Delap, Enoch Davis, J. A. Parks, Wm. Lambeth, Benjamin Churchill and R. S. Green, to hold their meetings, the fifth Sunday in every month that has five Sundays, with the Saturday before, at Lexington, to transact business.

10. On motion, agreed to hold the next annual meeting of this body, with Reeds Cross Roads Church, five miles west of Lexington, to commence on Friday before the fourth Sabbath, in August 1857.

11. On motion, appointed Bro. Wm. Turner, to preach the Introductory Sermon, and Bro. Wm. Lambeth, his alternate.

On motion, this Association request Bro. Turner, to preach a doctrinal discourse, choosing his subject.

12. On motion, the Association proceeded to the choice of Preachers to occupy the stand on the Sabbath, which resulted in the choice of Bro. James McDaniel, A. Weaver and Wm. Turner, and Bro. James McDaniel to preach a Missionary Sermon at 11 o'clock. A. M.—take up a collection for domestic mission in our midst.

13. On motion, adjourned until Monday morning at 9 o'clock. Prayer by Elder Wm. Lambeth.

SABBATH.

The Ministers appointed to preach on this day, met a large, respectable and orderly congregation, at 9 o'clock; Bro. Wm. Turner, preached from Joel the 2 chapter 13 verse. Bro. James McDaniel, of Fayetteville, followed from Zachriah 13 chapter 1st verse. A collection was then taken up amounting to $11,63 for the use of domestic missions, after a recess of one hour, or at 3 o'clock P. M. Bro. A. Weaver, preached from 2nd Kings, 5th chapter 12th verse, all of which was very interesting and satisfactory.

MONDAY MORNING, AUGUST 25th.

The Association met according to previous adjournment, and after prayer by Elder Amos Weaver, the Association proceeded to business in the following manner:

1. On motion, Bro. A. Weaver, reported on Sabbath Schools. (See letter D.) Report received and Committee discharged.

Committee on Church letters and state of Religion, reported. Report adopted and Committee discharged. (E)

On missions, reported. Report received and Committee discharged. (F)

On Bible and Publication Society, reported. (See G) Report adopted, Committee discharged, and also adopted the resolution.

On motion, agreed to give Bro. Williams time to write a report at home, on the Baptist State Convention, and confer with Bro. A. Weaver, one of the Committee, and attach the report to the Ministers.

2. On motion, the Association proceeded to the organization of a Bible and Publication Society, when they pro-proceed to elect their officers. See further proceedings.

3. On motion, appointed Bro. Wm. Turner, Missionary in the northern portion of this Association, relying on his field for support.

'Also' on motion, appointed Bro. Wm. Lambeth, Missionary in Rowan County, relying on his field for support, and Bro. A. Williams, to the Piney Meeting House.

4. On motion, proceeded to elect Bro. Wm. Turner, to preach the Missionary sermon, on Sabbath, at our next annual meeting, at 11 o'clock, A. M.

On motion, the Clerk is directed to write to the board of the Convention, requesting them to appoint A. Weaver, riding Missionary in the bounds of this Association.

And we appoint Bro. John C. Averitt, delegate to the Baptist State Convention.

5. On motion, the delegates proceeded to pledge for the Churches or individuals, the sum announced to their names, to raise a fund to pay our Missionary for the ensueing year, which is a part of his salary.

| | |
|---|---|
| Bro. William Coggin, for Lick Creek,................ | $10 00 |
| Isaac Kinney, E. Merrill, for Jersey,................. | 10.00 |
| Aquilla Jones, Abbotts Creek,...................... | 10.00 |
| For himself,.................................... | 5.00 |
| S. Newsom, do., Toms Creek,..................... | 7.50 |
| Jonathan Welsh, do.. James Town,................. | 6.00 |
| Benjamin May, do., Liberty,....................... | 6.00 |
| Abram Palmer, do., Holloway's,................... | 5.00 |
| S. M. Charles, do., New Friendship,............... | 5.00 |
| Eli Coggin, do., Big Creek........................ | 5.00 |
| T. A. Parks, for self or Church at Reed's Cross Roads... | 5.00 |
| Benjamin Churchill, for Greensborough,............ | 5.00 |
| | $83.50 |

6. *Resolved*, That the Association return their thanks to the brethren and friends for their liberality in supporting this Meeting during its Session.

7. We further authorize the Clerk to have 500 copies of the Minutes printed, and distribute them as usual.

8. On motion, we adjourn to the time and place of the next Session of this body, when a few, touching and appropriate remarks were made by elder John C. Averitt, and concluded with singing and prayer.

BENJAMIN LANIER, Moderator.
AZARIAH WILLIAMS, Clerk.

6

## CONSTITUTION OF AN ASSOCIATIONAL BIBLE SOCIETY.

In order that we may more systematically and effectually co-operate with the Baptist Bible Society of this State and the Bible Board of the Southern Baptist Convention, in the great work of circulating the Holy Scriptures in our own and other lands, we hereby form ourselves into a Bible Society to act in connexion with this Association, and adopt the following Constitution.

## CONSTITUTION.

ARTICLE I. This Society ohall be called the Bible Society of the Liberty Association.

OF MEMBERS.

ARTICLE II. This Society shall be composed of the following classes of persons :

1st. Of all the messengers sent up with funds from congregational or other local bible societies, which shall be entitled to one delegate for every five dollars sent up.

2nd. Of representatives of Churches, Missionary Societies, Sunday Schools, or any other bodies which shall send up funds, one delegate for every five dollars sent up.

3d. Of all persons who shall have paid five dollars or more, at any one time to this Society, or to any of its auxiliaries. Such persons shall be counted members for life.

4th. Of all persons who are present at any meeting of the Society and contribute the sum of fifty cents shall be considered members for the year.

ARTICLE III. The object of this Society shall be to aid in circulation of the Holy Scriptures in our own and other lands ; and the funds collected by us shall be sent up to the State Baptist Bible Society of our own State, or to the Bible Board of the Southern Baptist Convention at Nashville.

OF OFFICERS.

ARTICLE IV. The Officers of this Society shall be a President, three Vice Presidents, a Secretary and Treasurer, who shall perform the duties common to officers in similar organizations ; and shall be elected by a plurality of votes at each annual meeting ; and in case of a failure to elect, shall hold their places until another meeting.

OF MEETINGS.

ARTICLE V. The regular annual meetings of this Society shall be held at the same time and place with the meetngs of our Association, at which the following order of business shall be observed :

1st. The reports of the Treasurer and of the Board of Directors shall be read.

2d. A sermon, or other addresses suitable to the occasion, shall be delivered.

3d. An opportunity given to those present to become members, by subscribing or contributing to our funds, and a general collection taken up.

4th. Officers elected and speakers appointed for the next meeting. An adjourned meeting may be held at any time, or one may be called at any time, by the President or either of the Vice Presidents.

OF LIFE DIRECTORS.

ARTICLE VI. Any person who shall contribute to our funds the sum of twenty dollars, at any one time, or in two annual installments, shall be considered life directors, and with the officers of the Society, shall constitute a Board to attend to any business in the interests of the regular meetings.

ARTICLE VII. This Constitution may be altered or amended by a vote of two thirds of the members present at any regular meeting.

The Bible Society, after their organization proceeded to elect officers for the present year, which resulted as follows : A. Williams, President ; Isaac Kinney, first Vice President ; J. A. Parks, second Vice President ; Wm. Turner, third Vice President ; John C. Averitt, Secretary and Treasurer.

### LIFE MEMBERS.

A. Williams, J. A. Parks, Alexander Delap, Isaac Kinney, Benjamin Lanier.

## ANNUAL MEMBERS BY THE PAYMENT OF FIFTY CENTS.

J. C. Averitt, Aquilla Jones, John Teague, William Turner, John Redwine, John Charles, Aquilla Teague, A. O. P. Teague, Benjamin Churchill, Jonathan Welch.

Amount subscribed,..................................$30.00
Cash received,.........................................15.50
$14.50

Elder John C. Averitt, was apointed to deliver an address before the B. B. Society at our next annual Association.            A. WILLIAMS, President.

JOHN C. AVERITT, Secretary.

---

### REPORT OF COMMITTEE ON FINANCE.

Received from the Churches.....................$17.72½
Funds in the hand of the Treasurer.................. 1.50
Total on hand at the present....................$19.22½

### (A.)

*The Committee appointed at last Association on Home Missions and Colportage, beg leave to report—*

That they found some difficulty in geting a Minister to travel in the bounds of the Association, generally with no certain compensation. However, we engaged Elder Amos Weaver some time the past Spring to devote a portion of his time as Missionary and Colporteur within the bounds of our Association, to rely entirely on his field for his support. All of which is respectfully submitted, by

ABRAM PALMER, Chairman.

### (B.)

### MISSIONARY'S REPORT.

I have, since my selection by your Committee as Missionary and Colportuer for this Association, not been able to obtain books, and as such have done nothing in the way of Colportage.

I have spent, in preaching and travelling, some twelve to fifteen days; which, together with time set apart for the same purpose, but which was not required, owing to meeting not being continued as long as anticipated. Worked some two thirds of a month.

I have received from the Churches the following amounts, to wit:

```
From Hollowell's,.................... $3.50
  "    Lick Creek,.....................  6.75
  "    Big Creek,......................  6.90
  "    Liberty,........................  3.75
```

All of which is respectfully submitted, by
AMOS WEAVER, MISSIONARY.

(c.)

*The following Report submitted by William Turner,— Missionary at Waughtown—*

I have preached thirteen sermons, baptised five of that congregation, and received Ten dollars and sixty three cents compensation.

(D.)

## REPORT ON SABBATH SCHOOLS.

*The Committee on Sabbath Schools, beg leave to submit the following Report—*

In looking over the field of our operation, and surveying the numerous instrumentalities now within the Church of Christ, your Committee are of the deliberate opinion that few—if any—of the legitimate labours to which the Church is invited, are so full of hope, or promise so rich and so gracious a return as Sabbath Schools. Yet, your Committee, with regret, have to state that this inviting field lies with us almost wholy uncultivated. It was a circumstance regarded by St. Paul as exceedingly auspicious in the life of an imminent son of his in the Gospel, " That from a child, he had known the Holy Scriptures," and there is no means known to your Committee equal to a well conducted Sabbath School, to familiarize the young mind with the word of God.

Solomon says, "Train up a child in the way he should go, and when he is old, he will not depart therefrom."—It will be said, perhaps, that parental training is here alluded to. Be it so. Still, it is a most appalling truth,—that pious parental training is far from being general.—Perhaps, in few cases is this so perfectly attained to in the family, as to render the Sabbath School unnecessary;—while, in very many instances, the children and youth of our country must and will continue to grow up in the most deplorable ignorance and vice; and, consequently, become the pest of both, Church and State, who might, under proper moral culture, seasonably and judiciously applied, become ornaments to both. This defect in parental training can only be met by the Church, through the agency of the Sabbath School. And none can doubt that it is the legitimate and sacred duty of the Church to look after this thing. And even under the most favourable circumstances, it has been found that Sabbath Schools are of invaluable advantage in strengthening and in forming parental religious cultivation.

Again, it is believed that among the happy results that usually attend the labours of a well conducted Sabbath School, the reflex influence on those teachers and superintendants engaged in conducting them, is by no means the least of their results. In the whole range of divine obligation, God has graciously blended our duty with our instincts; and this principle is not less positive and operative in the matter under consideration. Those who engaged for any considerable length of time, heartily, in the delightful task of impressing the minds of our children and youth, with the duties of religion and obligations o f piety, cannot fail to have the sphere of their own knowledge of God—His law and government enlarged—their hearts enobled, and their Spiritual graces improved.—Thus, Sabbath Schools are in a two fold sense the nurseries of the Church—aiding and enforcing on the one hand parental efforts; and on the other, rendering powerful and effective, the living ministry, when it must, without them, be faintiless and inoperative. Your Committee, in view of the above facts and considerations, beg leave to offer the following Resolution and recommend its adoption :

*Resolved*, That this Association recommend each Church within our bounds to form Sabbath Schools at their respective Meeting Houses, or at such other place or places, as, they shall find most convenient, that they take such steps in regard to the same as to have their Schools regular organizations, and that they send up their Delegates to the next Association, with full return of their proceedings on this matter with authority to organize, during that meeting of our Body, an Associational Sabbath School Society, to which each, in our bounds, may act as auxiliary.

All of which is respectfully submitted.

AMOS WEAVER, Chairman.

(E.)

*The Committee on Church Letters and state of Religion Report—*

That from the statistics of the Churches in this Association, we find that during the past year, there has been little or no increase. Religion, then, must be in rather a low state. We are taught that when Zion travails, she brings forth : and it is manifest, from the experience of every one, that when the Church is in a luke-warm condition, that there is but little interest felt by the world in matters of religion. If the light of the Christian grows dim in the same proportion, darkness will pervade the earth, and sinners will press onward in the road to ruin ; for he that walketh in darkness, knoweth not whither he goeth. There is great responsibility resting upon us. We would say—first to the Ministry : "Cry aloud, spare not; lift thy voice like a trumpet, and show my people their transgressions, and the house of Jacob their sins." And secondly, to the laity, we say : Hold up your Ministers' hands ; let them feel, like a mighty engine, the power of your co-operation; and then you will see Zion prospering —for God works through his people; and the religion of Jesus Christ prompts us to act in this great Scheme of benevolence; and we know that our labour is not in vain with the Lord. The stone cut out without hands became a great Nation and filled the whole earth.

All of which is respectfully submitted.

WILLIAM TURNER, Chairman.

(f.)

REPORT ON MISSIONS.

The importance of Missions must be evident to those who are acquainted with the moral condition of the world. The majority of the inhabitants of the globe are still enveloped in Pagan darknes. The glad tidings of salvation through the mediation of Christ has never saluted their ears. It is not necessary, however, to look beyond our own bounds to see the importance of Missions. Even within the limits of Liberty Association, there are many sections almost entirely destitute of preaching of any kind and many other sections destitute of Baptist preaching.— It is to be feared that the Baptists, generally, have not viewed their obligations to disseminate divine truth in the proper light. If a field is occupied by some Protestant denomination, it is not regarded as Missionary ground.— This is a great mistake. Jesus Christ never planted but one Church in the world, and that was composed of immersed believers. To that Church he gave the commission: "Go ye, therefore, into all the world, and preach the Gospel to every creature." Upon this Church the obligation still rests to carry out this commission to its full extent. It is therefore not only our duty to send a Missionary to those places where there is no preaching, but it is also our duty to send a Missionary to those places where the ordinances are not kept as they were delivered by inspired Apostles, a man who is able and willing to defend the distinctive views of the Baptists, and to refute and expose peda-Baptist errors. If this course had been pursued faithfully, in time past, our views would have been generally known, and would have prevailed to a far greater extent. We have insisted chiefly on Missions within our bounds,, not with a view to under value the vast importance of Foreign Missions, but because we think that very little will be done for them unless the Home Missions are faithfully and successfully prosecuted. The most successful way to awaken an interest for Foreign Missions,—is to arouse the attention of our Churches to the importance of supplying their own destitution.— Having appointed a Missionary within our own limits, let us determine to sustain him by our prayers and our contributions. Brethren, let us endeavor to labour more and pray more for the advancement of the Redeemer's Kingdom; let us adopt the prayer of the dying Psalmist:— "Let the whole earth be filled with His glory. Amen, and Amen." Respectfully submitted. .

JOHN C. AVERITT, Chairman.

(G.)
## REPORT ON BAPTIST CONVENTION.

*Your Committee, to whom was refered the subject of the Convention, submit the following :*

The Convention was organized upwards of twenty-one years ago, by brethren, whose hearts yearned over dying men more than over this worlds goods. Whose chief object was then, and still is, of sending the Gospel to the destitute portions of our State, and to aid poor young preachers to obtain an education, to qualify them for the work of the Ministry—and send the Missionary to the land of Heathenism, with the blessed Gospel of the Son of God.

1. When we take a retrospective view of the moral darkness that still pervades our land, and the great destitution that pervades our Villages, Towns and Neighborhoods, for the bread of life, can we withhold any longer from aiding the Convention, in sending the Missionary

among those famishing Millions, whose cries are rising up before the Lord of Sabbaoth.

2. And when we leave our own beloved Country, and take a view of those idoldetrous nations, the heart sickens at the awful scenes that transpire. The Mother offering her tender offsprings to Idols, the wife bound to the Funeral pile of her husband, the infirm buried alive, the worshiping of gnats &c., &c., How can any withhold? Who has tested that the Lord is good, from aiding the Convention, in sending the Missionary, among them. Brethren, it requires more than a few empty wishes to accomplish the great work. How much owest thou the Lord? pay thy dues, as it will profit little to say be ye warmed, filled clothed, while ye withhold, the needful things.

3. The Convention has a great and glorious work to accomplish, and no agent in the field this year, but entirely depending on the Liberality of the brethren and friends for help. The Convention has not near enough Missionaries employed to supply the domestic mission, besides they need funds to sustain the beneficiaries already at Wake Forest. To sustain these, it requirers all the means at their command. While many men ought and desire to be there, they nor the Convention, have not the means, and hence the number is small, much has been done, but more remains to be done.

4. The education of the rising Ministry, is a subject of vital importance to the Church. Every other profession is crowded with educated men, and the ministry ought to keep pace with them, in order to instruct, and meet the evils of the infidel and deist. Now brethren permit us to solicit your prayers and alms, in behalf of the Convention, as North Carolina contains at this time, fifty thousand three hundred and twenty three Baptist, according to the last accounts. When we see how little is contributed according to membership, how can we say that we desire the salvation of our fellow being? and make so little or no sacrifice to accomplish it. Let every Baptist do like the

poor widow, in part, throw in their mite into the treasure of the Lord, don't wait for an agent to dun you, but send it up immediately to the Convention, and let those that refuse, ask themselves, have I done what I could, if so, well done thou good and faithful servant.

All of which is respectfully submitted.
ASARIAH WILLIAMS, CHAIRMAN.

(H.)

*The Committee to whom was submitted the Bible cause, present the following report—*

The conversion of the world, is obviously the great object for united christian effort. Among the means by which this object is to be attained, the circulation of the Bible, in the various languages of the people, is the most important. By God's Truth, men are to be reformed and converted. The entrance of this word giveth light.— "Sanctify them through thy Truth, thy word is Truth."

The circulation of the Bible is a work committed by God, to the Church. "Ye are the light of the world," so says the Saviour. They are not only to be lights in their character, exhibiting in their temper, spirit, disposition, and manner of living, the excellence of religion ; but they are, by christian effort, to circulate the Bible, this light which shines in a dark place, able to make men wise unto salvation. They are to hold forth the word of life to the nations of the earth. in this way.

The wants that exist for the Bible, in our own country, and in foreign lands, have been made known to this Association by the circular of the Southern Bible Board, which was read on Saturday. God, in his providence, has opened most of the countries to the circulation of the Bible, and a voice seems to call the church to go up and possess the land thus spread out before them.

Your Committee believe this Association to be capable of performing an importont part, in this department of christian duty. And they hope that some systematic plan of operation, in aid of this cause, will be adopted at this session, convinced as they are, that the time for action has fully come. They beg leave to present, therefore, the following resolution for the consideration of the Association.

*Resolved*, That this Association organize an Associational Bible Society, to aid in the circulation of the Scriptures.

All of which is respectfully submitted.

JAMES McDANIEL, CHAIRMAN.

## LIST OF ORDAINED PREACHERS BELONGING TO THIS ASSOCIATION.

Alfred Kinney, of Lick Creek; Benjamin Lanier, of Tom's Creek; Amos Weaver, of Jersey; A. Williams, of Reed's Cross Roads; William Turner, of New Friendship; William Lambeth, and John C. Averitt, of Salisbury; Orin Churchill, of James Town.

LICENTIATES.—Green Tussey, Aaron Yarborough and John A. Cornish, of Reed's Cross Roads; William R. Coggin and John Redwine, of Lick Creek.

## Tabular View of the Churches.

| County. | Post Office. | By Whom supplied. | Delegates' Names. | Baptised. | Rec'd by Letter. | Restored. | Dis. by Letter. | Excluded. | Deceased. | White. | Colored. | Total. | Funds $ cts. | Ch. Members. |
|---|---|---|---|---|---|---|---|---|---|---|---|---|---|---|
| Davidson. | Jackson Hill, | A KINNEY | J Adderton, Wm R Coggin, John Redwine, | 18 | 2 | | 1 | 1 | 2 | 81 | | 81 | 1 90 | 48 |
| Davidson. | Cotton Grove, | A WEAVER. | A Weaver, J Kinny, Ebenezer Merrill, | 4 | 1 | | 3 | 9 | 9 | 108 | 145 | 253 | 3 00 | 1 |
| Montgomery. | Abbotts Creek, | WM TURNER. | A Jones, William Clinard, John Teague, | | 3 | | | 2 | 1 | 91 | 2 | 93 | 2 00 | 3 |
| Davidson. | Healing Springs | B LANIER. | John Skeen, S. Sheets, Sampson Newsom, | 5 | | | 2 | | | 26 | 4 | 30 | 1 00 | 3 |
| Guilford. | James Town, | B LANIER. | J Welch, G. W. Johnson, B. Harris, | | | | 3 | 1 | | 24 | | 24 | 1 00 | 4 |
| Davidson. | Fair Grove, | A WEAVER. | B. May, S S Lambeth, K. Miller, | | | | | 1 | 2 | 48 | 1 | 49 | 1 00 | 38 |
| Davidson. | Silver Hill, | A KINNEY. | A. Palmer, C Smith, F. Beanblossom, | 7 | 2 | | 2 | | 2 | 45 | 28 | 73 | 75 | 2 |
| Forsyth. | Waugh Town, | WM TURNER. | S M Charles, J. Syres, R. Y. Charles, | 4 | 1 | | 2 | | | 44 | | 44 | 1 00 | 2 |
| Montgomery. | Wind Hill, | B LANIER. | D Coggin, S. R. Coggin, Ira Hambleton. | 1 | | | | | 2 | 46 | 4 | 50 | 1 00 | 2 |
| Davidson. | Lexington, | B LANIER. | *Report given by Bro'er A. Williams. | | | | | | 2 | 8 | | 10 | 87½ | 2 |
| Davidson. | Lexington, | WM LAMBETH. | A Yarborough, J. H. Owen, I. A. Park, | 2 | | | 5 | 1 | 1 | 69 | 3 | 72 | 1 50 | 28 |
| Davidson. | Lexington, | WM LAMBETH. | | 1 | 1 | | 1 | | | 15 | 3 | 18 | | 48 |
| Rowan. | Salisbury, | J. C AVERITT. | William Lambeth, J. C. Averitt. | | 3 | | | | 1 | 44 | | 44 | 1 00 | 38 |
| Guilford. | Greensborough, | O. CHURCHILL, | Jonas Lineberry, John Ingold, Benj. Churchill, | 3 | 1 | | | | | 32 | | 32 | 1 00 | 1 |
| | | | | 44 | 9 | 3 | 19 | 4 | 21 | 681 | 299 | 980 | 17 72½ | |

REED'S CROSS ROADS M. H., DAVIDSON CO.,
FRIDAY, AUGUST 21ST, 1857.

The members of Liberty Association met according to adjournment. The Introductory Sermon, in the absence of br. Wm. Turner, was delivered by br. WM. LAMBETH, from Rom. 2nd chapt.; 6th verse.

1. After a short intermission, the members met again. The Association, in the absence of our former Moderator, was called to order by br. A. Weaver, acting as Moderator pro tem. Letters handed in and contents noted. See last page.

2. The Delegates present proceeded to elect a Moderator for the present term, which resulted in the choice of br. AMOS WEAVER.

On motion, the Letter from Greensborough was received, and br. Ingole and Churchwell received as Delegates.

3. On motion, Rev. E. Dodson, from Bulah, Agent for Southern Board of Foreign Missions of N. C.; and Rev R. H. Griffith, C. W. Bessent, and C. W. Tatum, correspondents from the Yadkin Association, were cordially received, by the Moderator extending the hand of fellowship.

4. On motion of br. Wm. Lambeth, the Moderator appointed br. Jonathan Welsh, Eli Davis, and Aquilla Jones, with the Moderator and Clerk, a Committee of Arrangements, during the meeting, and brn. Wm. Owen and Alexander Delap, a Committee of Finance.

5. On motion, appointed the Delegates and Pastor of Reed's Cross Roads, to act as Committee to arrange religious services during this meeting, except on the Sabbath.

6. On motion, the Association gave away for the Bible Society, at 2 o'clock on Saturday; and br. E. Dodson appointed to deliver an address.

On motion adjourned until to-morrow, 9 o'clock, A. M. Prayer by Elder R. H. Griffith.

## SATURDAY, AUGUST 22ND.

Met according to previous adjournment. Religious services by br. R. H. Griffith.

1. On motion, Committee of Arrangements reported. The Report received and the Committee continued.

2. Invited transient Ministers and Licentiates to take seats : Wm. H. Davis from the Yadkin came forward and took a seat with us.— Br. E. F. Eaton came forward as a correspondent from the Yadkin, and was received.

3. Appointed Elders R. H. Griffith, C. W. Bessent, and E. Dodson, a standing committee on Resolutions.

4. Called on correspondents to Sister Associations to report : Elder Wm. Turner attended the Yadkin, was cordially received, and had an interesting meeting. Elder A. Weaver reported, that he and the brethren appointed, attended the Sandy Creek Association, and gave an interesting account of that body, and their progress. Br. Redwine attended the Pee Dee; but the rest were not present to report. Those appointed to attend the Bulah, gave a satisfactory excuse for not attending.

4. On motion, the Report of the Correspondents received, and those that failed to attend, were excused.

5. On motion, appointed Correspondents to Sister Associations :— To the Yadkin, Elder Wm. Turner and brn. Wm. R. Coggin and R.

J. Charles; to be held at the East Bend. To Sandy Creek, commencing on Friday before the 1st Sabbath in October; Elder A. Weaver, brn. Wm. Owen, and A. Palmer; to be held in Chatham County, 14 miles S. W. of Pittsboro', at Bear Creek Church. To Pee Dee, to be held in Anson County, Pine M. H.; Elder B. Lanier, br. John Redwine, and br. Eli Davis. To Buelah, to be held at Cane Creek, about 10 miles S. W. of Hillsborough, commencing on Friday before the 2nd Sabbath in August, 1858; Elder A. Weaver, Wm. Lambeth, and brn. John Teague, James Smith, and Wm. Owen.

6. Called on Board of Missions to report:—Three of the Board reported that they had one meeting, employed Elder A. Weaver, paid over the funds, and held no more meetings. The Report received and Board dismissed.

7. Called on Missionaries to report: When Elders A. Weaver, A. Williams, Wm. Turner, and Wm. Lambeth reported. The Reports received and ordered to be attached to the Minutes. [See Appendix, A, B, C, D.

8. On motion, the Association recommend the Greensboro' Church, worshiping at Cumberland, to purify themselves; and we tender the services of Elder A. Weaver, if requested, to aid in the same.

9. On motion, agreed to have the Churches comprizing each District, printed, or attached to the Minutes.

10. On motion, agreed to hold the next annual meeting of this body with Holloways Church, 10 miles S. E. of Lexington, to commence on Friday before the fourth Sabbath in August, 1858.

On motion, appointed Elder A. Weaver to preach the Introductory Sermon; and br. Wm. Turner, his alternate.

On motion, appointed Elder B. Lanier to preach a Missionary Sermon; Wm. Turner his alternate.

11. On motion, appointed the following Committees: On Church Letters and State of Religion, Elder Wm. Lambeth, Wm. R. Coggin and B. Churchill. On Sabbath Schools, Elder R. H. Griffith, Ebenezer Merrell, Wm. Clinard and John Cornish. On Missions, Home and Foreign, Elder Wm. Turner, Aquilla Jones, and R. J. Charles. On Bible and Publication Society, Elder C. W. Bessent, Enoch Davis and S. W. Lanier. On Periodicals, Elder E. Dodson, John Teague, and Wm. Owen. On Colportage, Elder E. Dodson, C. W. Bessent and A. Williams. On Temperance, B. F. Eaton, B. Churchill, and John Cornish. On Baptist State Convention, Elder R. H. Griffith, brn. Wm. Owen and Pinkney Redwine. On Education, A. Williams, A. Delap, and R. S. Green.

12. On motion, adjourned until 3 o'clock, P. M. Prayer by Elder Wm. Turner.

Met according to adjournment. Prayer by Elder E. Dodson.

13. On motion, the Report on Missions received, and Committee discharged. [Letter E.]

14. On motion, the Committee on Finance reported that they had received from the churches, $18 37. Report received, and Committee discharged.

15. On motion, the Resolutions offered on Colportage and on Minister's and Deacons Meetings, were referred to the Committee on Resolutions.

16. On motion, the Association proceeded to the choice of preachers to occupy the stand on the Sabbath, which resulted in the choice

## SABBATH.

The Ministers appointed to preach on this day, met an unusually large, respectable and orderly congregation. At 10 o'clock, Elder C. W. Bessent preached from Matthew, the 25th chapter and 13th verse. Elder Wm. Turner followed at 11 o'clock, from John, the 6th chapter 27th verse. A public collection was taken up for Domestic Missions in the bounds of the Association, amounting to $22 25.

After a recess of one hour, or at 3 o'clock, P. M., Elder R. H. Griffith preached from I Peter, 3rd chapter and 15th verse,—all of which were edifying and interesting to the attentive hearer.

## MONDAY MORNING, AUGUST 24th, 1857.

1. The Association met according to adjournment. And after religious services by br. Jno. A. Cornish, the Association proceeded to business, in the following manner:

2. The standing Committee on Resolutions reported; and after several interesting speeches by Elders Dodson, Griffith, Weaver and others, the Resolutions were read, adopted, and ordered to be annexed to the Minutes.

Resolved, That we recommend this Association to revive Ministers and Deacon's Meetings at times and places most convenient.

Resolved, That we recommend the Churches within our bounds to send up in their letters to the Association the amount paid to their Pastors.

3. The Committee on Church Letters and State of Religion reported:—Report received and Committee discharged. [See H.]

4th. The Committee on Sabbath Schools, reported: Report received and Committee discharged. [See I.]

5. The Committee on Temperance reported: Report read and adopted, and committee discharged. [See J.]

6. The Committee on Education reported: Report adopted.—[See K.]

7. On motion, the following Resolution was adopted:

Resolved, That we request our Pastors to act as colporteurs within their respective fields, during the ensuing year; and to aid them in this matter, we appoint a Board consisting of the following persons, to wit: James Wiseman, Wm. Owen, Henry Smith, A. Palmer and J. A. Parks; three of whom may form a quorum to procure the Books and furnish the several Pastors with the same.

8. On motion, a Committee of one member from each Church represented, report the following arrangements for Minister's and Deacon's Meetings in the following manner, viz:

Big Creek, Lick Creek and Tom's Creek to compose the 1st District. Holloways, Jersey and Salisbury the 2nd. Reed's Cross Roads, Marion, Pine Meeting House, and Liberty, the 3rd. And Abbott's Creek, Jamestown, Greensborough and New Friendship, the 4th.— The first meeting to be held with Lick Creek Church, commencing on Saturday before the fifth Sabbath after August, and be held regularly in each District on the fifth Sabbath.

9. On motion, the Report of the Committee on Periodicals received and committee discharged. [See L.]

10. On motion, called on the Treasurer to report:

For printing Minutes and Postage, $12 22
Clerk's allowance for last year, 5 00

Amount, 17 22
On hand last year, 19 22

In accordance with a motion of the Association, we give an account of the Churches composing the three Districts of the Accociation :—1st Section, New Friendship, Abbots Creek, Jamestown, and Greensboro'. 2nd, Jersey, Liberty, Pine Meeting House, Marion, Reed's Cross Roads, and Salisbury. 3rd, Holloways, Tom's Creek, Lick Creek and Big Creek.

11. *Resolved*, That this Association return their thanks to the brethren and friends for their liberality in supporting this meeting during its session.

12. We further authorize the Clerk to have 500 copies of the Minutes printed, and distribute them as usual.

13. On motion, we adjourn to the time and place of the next session of this Body, when a few very feeling and appropriate remarks were made by the Moderator, and concluded with singing and prayer.

AMOS WEAVER, *Moderator.*

Azariah Williams, *Clerk.*

## A.--Report of Missionaries.

I spent three months in your service, labored, I know not how much, and kept no account of the distance traveled; but know that I labored to the extent and even beyond my ability. I witnessed the Baptism of three at Lick Creek, and several at New Friendship, and had interesting meetings, at various places.

I received from the churches and others, the following sums, viz : From an individual at Abbott's Creek, 25 cts. do. at Kendals, $5 00. Lick Creek, $10 00. Columbia, $1 20. New Friendship, $3 95. Tom's Creek, $1 00. Rev. B. Lanier and family, $2 25. Jersey, $10 00. Holloway's, $5 00. Greensboro', B. Churchill, $5 00. Br. Jonathan Welsh, $3 25. Br. J. A. Parks, $1 75. A. Williams, Clerk, $11 63. Abbott's Creek, $10 00.

Total receipts from churches and others, $70 08.

All of which is respectfully submitted,

AMOS WEAVER.

(B.)—Dear Brethren :—Permit me, as your Missionary to the Pine Meeting House, to submit the following report :

I have attended that church monthly, since last Association, with preaching whenever the weather and my health admitted ; administered the Lord's Supper once ; and received fifty cents from one individual. I took up no public collection.

I find there considerable opposition from our opposing brethren, yet the congregations are serious and respectful, and there is a prospect of good being done.

All of which is respectfully submitted. A. WILLIAMS.

(C.)—Rev. Wm. Turner's Report, as Missionary in the Northern part of the Liberty Association.

I have traveled several miles, (took no account,) and preached twenty-two sermons ; Baptised 1 or 12, &c.,—only one properly in the Missionary field. Received about three dollars remuneration:—Winston conventional operations and pastoral services not included.

WM. TURNER.

(D.)—Dear Brethren: The following is my report, as Missionary to the Count of Rowan.

## E. Report on Missions.

*The Committee on Missions beg leave to submit the following report:*
The field of Missions embraces the destitute parts of our Association, of the State, of the 20 Southern States, and of the World.

The wants of North Carolina should be supplied

Our Southern States have destitution. As many as 500,000 foreigners are coming yearly into America. The New States are principally their homes. In China there are eighteen States with different dialects; but when words are *written* all understand them. More than 75,000,000 have rebelled in the very heart of China, and their commander is opposed to Idolatry. The African Mission is very prosperous. The fields enlarging, are demanding more prayers and more sacrifices.

### EXAMPLES OF BENEVOLENCE.

The English Baptists give $1 for each member, to Foreign Missions. The Goshen Association, in Virginia, with a membership of 10,269, gives $5.571 58 cts., yearly, or 54 cents per member, to our various Boards. She has six Missionaries and two Colporteurs in and out of her bounds, in Virginia. Besides what she does in Virginia, she gives yearly, $2,860 for Foreign Missions. She has a Sabbath School in almost every church. She realizes the promise, "they that wait upon the Lord, shall renew their strength."

The Dan River Association, in Virginia, 20 odd miles below Danville, and numbering, in 1856, 1,697 members, gave in that year to our various Boards, $1,038 11 cts., or 61 cents to each member. If the Liberty Association of 980 members would give the same, the amount for the Home, Bible, and Foreign Boards would be $597.80 cts.

SYSTEM.—If every member would give one-tenth of his gross income, or as much as a pious Jew gave 3,000 years ago, the sum could be raised. God has a system in creation, and without system nothing definite can be done.

INFORMATION.—The Commission, and the Home and Foreign Journal are the organs. Both are printed monthly in Richmond, Va., The price of the first is $1 and of the second 25 cents.

The gospel is *aggressive*, and is designed to cover the whole earth.

Respectfully submitted,

---

The Bible Society held a meeting on Saturday August the 22nd, at 3 o'clock; (the Association gave away at this hour;) and after their organization, proceeded to elect officers for the present year, which resulted as follows: A. WILLIAMS, *President.* ISAAC KENNEY, 1st *Vice President;* J. A. PARKS, 2nd *Vice President;* WM. TURNER, 3rd *Vice President.* AMOS WEAVER, *Secretary and Treasurer.*

### LIFE MEMBERS.

A. Williams, J. A. Parks, Alexander Delap, and Catharine Delap, Isaac Kinney, B. Lanier, Dr. W. H. Wiseman.

*Annual members, by the payment of fifty cents.*

Amos Weaver, John A. Cornish, Gersham Tussey, James Wiseman, Benjamin Churchill, Ebenezer Merrell, George Byerly, Jacob Kimble, E. W. Tatum, Wm. Owen, George Riley.

Amount given by Life members, $10 00
Annual members 5 50

*The Committee on Church Letters and State of Religion report :—*

That from the statistics of the churches in this Association, we find that during the past year, there has been little or no increase in our numerical strength. Religion seems to be at a very low state within our bounds. We ask, why does this state of things exist?—The Lord's arm is not shortened, nor is he deaf, that he cannot hear. We believe that it is now as it was in the days of the prophet,—that the sins of the people have separated them from their God.

Brethren, we would call your earnest attention to this subject, that you may devise some remedy, under the blessing of God, that this coldness may be removed. Brethren, we have been writing reports and passing resolutions long enough. Come, let us awake to our duty, and use every means God has placed within our reach for the building up of the weak points within our bounds. The Committee would recommend those churches that complain of having no pastor, to do their duty in this matter, and God will soon send them an under shepherd to go in and out before them. All of which is respectfully submitted.　　　　　　　　　　WM. LAMBETH, *Chairman.*

## I. Report on Sabbath Schools.

When we look at the institution of the Sabbath School, we must pronounce it a good one, because God has blessed it as a means of bringing many souls to the knowledge of the gospel of the Son of God. There is much destitution in the bounds of this Association, and therefore we advise the brethren to look after those destitute places, and organize schools in every quarter. Solomon says:—"Train up a child in the way he should go, and when he is old he will not depart therefrom." There are hundreds of children in the bounds of this Association who are growing up without the proper bible instruction; therefore let us labor in the vineyard of the Lord, that proper principles may be instilled into their youthful minds. The Sabbath School hath many charms. Organize schools in the desert, and it will flourish and blossom as the rose. All of which is respectfully submitted.
　　　　　　　　　　J. A. CORNISH, *Chairman.*

## J. Temperance.

*The Committee on Temperance, beg leave to report :*

The subject of Temperance does not receive that consideration which its importance demands. The church as well as the world, seems too much disposed to close its eyes to the misery which intemperance is causing in society. When we look around us, we see an apparent indifference on this subject, which is sad to behold. It will hardly be necessary to go into an argument to prove that intemperance is a great evil,—a great sin ; or that it is lamentably prevalent in society. It is a matter for devout gratitude to God, that its ravages are less at present than at some former periods ; while it is a source of grief that it is even now affecting around us, and in our midst, miseries heart rending to contemplate. No grade in society, no profession has escaped its withering blight.

How many young men of the finest talents and fairest prospects have been ruined by it? How many loving wives and doting mother's have been made to drink to the bottom the most bitter cup of sorrow? How many happy family circles have been plunged into grief? How many fathers, proud of the opening prospects of noble sons, have had their hopes crushed, laid, been made to go mourning all their days, in sadness and sorrow ?—All because of intemperance.

grasp is death ?

But these are only the considerations that relate to time. When we lift the veil, and look into the eternal world, the words, "No drunkard shall inherit the kingdom of Heaven," being the light by which we see into the future state, alas! alas! how appalling the sight! the soul sickens and turns from the sight. We see hell peopled with the victims of that curse to the human family, strong drink. What christian's heart is not moved by such a sight? Where is the christian heart that is not prompted by the love of souls, the love of Jesus, to put forth the hand and arrest the unfortunate victim of intemperance in his mad career, and to lift a voice of entreaty, beseaching him to stop, ere it is too late; and to afford all the help in his power to effect the needed reformation?

Brethren, how can this be done? How will you do it? By closing your eyes to the danger; by setting the example yourselves and indulging in drinking strong drink; by making it an article of trade or engaging in the work of selling it? We ask, in the name and for the sake of immortal souls, is this the way you will arrest the progress of this soul destroying evil in our midst? God Almighty forbid. It is time for us to awake out of sleep on this subject; it is high time the church was exerting itself to eradicate the monster evil from our midst.

Let us, brethren, take a bold, and God-helping, an immovable stand in this matter. All of which is respectfully submitted.

B. F. EATON, *Chairman.*

### K. Report on Education.

The subject of education is one which commends itself to an enlightened community; but its moral bearing is so manifest, as to merit the fostering care of the christian church. Hence the advocates of pure christianity have always been the efficient promoters of education. It is manifest that it will not do for christians to stand aloof from the great interest and suffer it to fall under the exclusive control of those who have little or no regard for the moral or religious training of the rising generation.

We rejoice to see the Baptist denomination taking so much interest in this good and great enterprise. We hope that the day is not far distant when every parent will be awakened to his duty in this matter, especially every christian father and mother. For it is the opinion of your committee, that no parent discharges the obligations God has imposed upon him or her, who fails to use every possible means to give his or her children a good education. It gives to an individual an influence which nothing else can impart. A young gentleman or lady with a good education, may soon acquire influence, and do much more to benefit society than one with a fortune, but uneducated. We think this should cause every parent to stretch every nerve to give his son or daughter that intellectual training which will command respect wheresoever they may go.

Brethren, you know where our denominational schools are, male and female. Then send your sons and daughters. All of which is respectfully submitted. A. WILLIAMS, *Chairman.*

### L. Periodicals.

Your Committee would recommend the Biblical Recorder to all our members. It ought to have 5,000 instead of 2,500 subscribers. A general effort would secure the result. The Home and Foreign Journal at 25 a year, and the Commission at $1 a year, ought to be in every family to give light on our three General Boards. Both are monthly and come from Richmond, Va., one at $1 per year and the other at 25 cents. The

# A Tabular View of the Churches.

| CHES. | COUNTIES. | POST OFFICES. | BY WHOM SUPPLIED. | DELEGATES' NAMES. | Baptized | Rec. by Lett. | Restored | Dis. by Lett. | Excluded | Deceased | Whites. | Colored. | Total Num. | Fund | Q. Meet. Sa. |
|---|---|---|---|---|---|---|---|---|---|---|---|---|---|---|---|
| ek. | Davidson, | Jackson Hill, | Alfred Kinney | Jas. Adderton, Jos. Carreck, Pinkney Redwine, | 3 | 1 | | | 2 | | 77 | 2 | 79 | 2 00 | 4 |
| | do | Cotton Grove, | Amos Weaver, | Henry Smith, Wm. Owen, Ebenezer Merrell, | 11 | 1 | | | 5 | 2 | 103 | 46 | 149 | 3 92 | 3 |
| Creek, | do | Abbott's Creek, | Wm. Turner, | Aquilla Jones, Wm. Clinard, John Teague, | | | | 1 | 1 | | 149 | 3 | | 1 50 | 3 |
| reek, | do | Healing Springs, | B. Lanier, | Peter Riley, Simeon Sheets, Samuel Lanier, | 1 | | | | | | 85 | 252 | | 1 00 | 3 |
| wn, | Guildford; | Jamestown, | No supply, | Jonathan Welch, Branson Harris, | | | | 4 | 1 | 1 | 25 | 4 | 29 | 1 00 | 1 |
| | Davidson, | Jamestown, | No supply, | John Fine, Kinley Miller, Wagoner Miller, | | 3 | | | | | 21 | | 21 | 75 | 4 |
| y's, | do | Fair Grove, | Alfred Kinney | Frederick Beanblossom, John Cross, Chas. Smith, | 1 | | | | | | 45 | 21 | 46 | 75 | 4 |
| | Forsyth, | Silver Hill, | Wm. Turner, | Alexander Delap, R. J. Charles, Jesse Styers, | 2 | 2 | 1 | 4 | | 1 | 45 | 28 | 73 | 1 00 | 2 |
| endship. | do | Waughtown, | Wm. Turner, | E. H. Davis, Eli Davis, Wm. Hamilton, | 12 | 2 | | | 4 | | 28 | | 53 | 2 00 | 2 |
| k. | Montgomery, | Wind Hill, | B. Lanier, | Represented by A. Williams, | 1 | 1 | | 2 | 1 | | 53 | | 53 | 1 00 | 2 |
| House, | Davidson, | Lexington, | A. Williams, | Daniel S. Hunt, Aaron Yarbrough, Alfred Wood, | | | | | 4 | | 47 | 4 | 51 | 1 10 | 2 |
| Roads, | do | do | A. Williams, | R. S. Green, A. Williams, | 2 | 1 | | 2 | 1 | | 8 | 2 | 10 | 50 | 4 |
| | do | do | Wm. Lambeth, | | 2 | 1 | | 9 | 2 | | 69 | 3 | 72 | 1 70 | 2 |
| | do | Salisbury, | R. S. Green, | | 1 | | | 10 | | 1 | 8 | 11 | 11 | 50 | 3 |
| rough. | Rowan, | Greensborough, | Wm. Lambeth | A. Williams, | | | | | 4 | | 41 | 1 | 52 | 1 25 | 1 |
| | Guilford, | | No supply, | Jonathan P. Ingole, Benjamin Churchill. | 1 | | | 1 | 1 | | 19 | | 19 | 1 00 | |
| | | | | | 33 | 6 | 1 | 24 | 13 | 23 | 656 | 199 | 855 | 18 47 | |

OF ORDAINED PREACHERS BELONGING TO THIS ASSOCIATION:—Wm. N. Hereford and Alfred Kinney, of Lick Creek; Benjamin of Tom's Creek; Amos Weaver, of Jersey; A. Williams, of Reed's Cross Roads; Wm. Turner, of New Friendship; Wm. Lambeth, ury; Orin Churchill, of Jamestown.

TIATES.—Gersham Tussey, Aaron Yarbrough, and John A. Cornish, of Reed's Cross Roads; Wm. R. Coggin, and John Redwine, of ek.

# MINUTES

## OF THE TWENTY–SIXTH SESSION

### OF THE

# Liberty Baptist Association,

### HELD AT

## HOLLOWAY'S MEETING-HOUSE,

### DAVIDSON COUNTY, N. C.,

### *August the 20th, 21st and 23rd, 1858.*

---

HOLLOWAY'S M. H., DAVIDSON COUNTY, N. C. }
*Friday, August 20th, 1858.* }

The members of the Liberty Association met according to adjournment. The introductory sermon was delivered by A. WEAVER,
from Matthew 21, 3: "The Lord hath need of him."

1. After a short intermission, the members met again. The
Association was called to order by Elder A. Weaver, former Moderator. Religious services by Elder Wm. Turner. Letters handed in
and contents noted. See last page.

2. The delegates proceeded to elect a Moderator for the present
term, which resulted in the choice of br. Amos Weaver.

3. Called on Correspondents from Sister Associations to come forward and take seats with us.

On motion, invited transient ministers to take seats; br. John A.
Conner accepted a seat, when brn. E. L. Parker and S. S. Stone
came forward from the Pedee Association, and were welcomed by the
Moderator extending the right hand of fellowship.

4. On motion, a Committee of Arrangements appointed, consisting of Elder Wm. Turner, John Teague, Elder A. Kinney, Eli Coggin and A. Palmer, with the Moderator and Clerk.

5. On motion of br. Turner, the Moderator appointed br. A. Delap
and J. A. Park a Committee of Finance.

6. On motion, appointed the delegates of Holloway's Church, a
Committee to arrange religious services during the meeting, except
Sabbath.

On motion, the Association gave away to the Bible Society, on
Saturday, 2 o'clock, P. M.

On motion, the Association adjourned until Saturday 9 o'clock.—
Religious services by Elder A. Kinney.

Met according to previous adjournment. Religious services by the Moderator, and prayer by Elder Gilbert.

1. On motion, the report of the Committee of Arrangements read. Report received and committee continued.

Invitation extended to corresponding brn. from sister Associations, when br. A. J. Gilbert, from Sandy Creek, came forward and was cordially received by the Moderator extending the right hand of fellowship.

2. On motion of br. J. A. Cornish, a standing Committee on Resolutions and Queries were appointed, consisting of Elders Wm. Turner, B. Lanier and A. Palmer.

3. On motion, called on correspondents to sister Associations to report: Elder Wm. Turner reported that he attended the Yadkin, and gave an interesting account of their progress. The brethren appointed to Sandy Creek and Bulah Associations, rendered satisfactory reasons for their failure, and were excused by the body.

4. On motion, proceeded to appoint correspondents to sister Associations: To the Yadkin to be held at Sandy Springs, commencing on Thursday before the 1st Sabbath in October, br. Jesse H. Owen, Elder Wm Turner and br. J. A. Cornish. To Sandy Creek, commencing on Friday before the 1st Sabbath in October, held at Love's Creek Church, 15 miles West of Pittsborough, Elder A. Weaver, A. Williams, and br. J. R. Nichols. To Pedee, to be held at Kendall's Church, commencing on Friday before the third Sabbath in October, Elders B. Lanier, A. Kinney and br. Wm. R. Coggin.— To the Bulah, to be held at the Elm Grove Church, Guilford County, commencing on Friday before the second Sabbath in August, 1859, Elders A. Weaver, Wm. Turner, brn. John Teague and J. Welch.

5. On motion, appointed the following Committees, to wit: On State of Religion and Church Letters, brn. Jesse H. Owen, Jesse Seabrist and M. Redwine. On Sabbath Schools, Charles Teague, J. A. Park and S. W. Lanier. On Home and Foreign Missions, Elder Wm. Turner, Ebenezer Merrell and John Teague. On Bibles, Publications and Periodicals, J. A. Park, J. R. Nichols and J. Rouch. On Colportage, John A Cornish, Elder A. Kinney and A. Delap.— On Temperance, Charles Teague, James W. Craver and P. W. Raper. On Education, A. Williams, Wm. Turner and A. Palmer.

6. On motion, rescinded the resolution of last year, requiring the churches to send the amount paid their pastors.

7. Called off until 4 o'clock, P. M. Prayer by the Moderator.

8. Resumed business again. Prayer by A. Williams.

9. The Association, on motion, proceeded to elect preachers to occupy the stand on Sabbath, which terminated in the choice of Elders A. Weaver and Wm. Turner.

10. On motion, the Treasurer reported funds on hand for Missionary purposes taken up last year, amounting to $22 25 cents.

The Association Fund.—After deducting all expenses, there remains $4 02 cents on hand.          A. WILLIAMS, *Treasurer.*

On motion, report received.

11. On motion, the Association allowed br. A. Williams, $12 of missionary fund for services rendered at P. M. House, for two years.

12. On motion, agreed to hold the next annual meeting of this Association with the New Friendship Church, Forsyth County, commencing on Friday before the 4th Sabbath in August, 1859.

13. On motion, appointed Elder B. Lanier to preach the introductory sermon; Elder A. Kinney, his alternate.

14. On motion, appointed Elder A. Weaver to preach the Missionary sermon on Sabbath.

15. On motion, appointed Elder Wm. Turner, S. Sheets and E. H. Davis a Committee on Baptist State Convention.

On motion, adjourned until Monday 9 o'clock, A. M.

## SABBATH

The ministers appointed to occupy the stand, met a large and orderly congregation. At 10 o'clock, Elder Amos Weaver preached from Hebrews, 2nd ch., 3rd v: "How shall we escape, if we neglect so great salvation." At 11 o'clock, Elder B. Lanier preached the Missionary sermon from II Corinthians, 8th ch, 9th v: "For ye know the grace of our Lord Jesus Christ, that though he was rich, for your sakes he became poor, that ye through his poverty might be rich." After which a public collection was taken up for Domestic Missions in the bounds of the Association, amounting to $16 11 cts.

After a recess of one hour or more, at 3 o'clock, P. M., Elder Wm. Turner preached from Isaiah, 25th chapter, 6th 7th and 8th v. "And in this mountain shall the Lord of hosts make unto all people a feast of fat things," &c. All of which were interesting and commanded respect.

## MONDAY MORNING, AUGUST 23rd, 1858.

The Association met according to adjournment. And after religious services by the Moderator, the Association proceeded to business in the following manner, viz:

1. On motion, the Committee on Finance reported that they had received from the churches, $14 40. Money handed over to the Treasurer. Report received and Committee discharged.

2. On motion, adopted the report on Sabbath Schools, and Committee discharged. (see A.)

3. On motion, adopted the Report on Home and Foreign Missions, and committee discharged. (see B.)

4. On motion, adopted the report on Bible publication and Periodicals, and committee discharged. (see C.)

5. On motion, adopted the report on colportage, and committee discharged. (see D.)

6. On motion, adopted the report on Temperance, and committee discharged. (see E.)

7. On motion, adopted the report on Baptist State Convention, and Committee discharged. (see F.)

8. On motion, adopted the report on Education, and committee discharged. (See G.)

9. On motion, adopted the Report on State of Religion and Church Letters, and committee discharged. (see H.)

The Committee on Resolutions report as follows:

1. *Resolved*, That the principles embodied in the old Landmark, reset by J. M. Pendleton, of Tennessee, are correct and should govern Baptists in relation to other denominations.

2. *Resolved*, That, in our judgment, the contrary would be a virtual surrender of our distinctness as a denomination, and constitute us no longer the true witnesses of Christ, or defenders of the faith as it

was once delivered to the saints, as we believe. true Baptists have ever been.　　　　　　　WM. TURNER, *Chairman*.

10. On motion, the memorial presented to the Association was received and ordered to be attached to the minutes, with the advice to Reed's Cross Road Church.  (see I.)

11. On motion, a Committee was appointed to go on the ground, examine into the condition of the Greensborough church, and report to the next Association.  The following compose said committee :— Jonathan Welch, John Teague and William Clinard.

12. On motion, ordered the Clerk to superintend the printing of the Minutes, 500 in number, and distribute them as usual.

13. *Resolved*, That this Association return their thanks to the brethren and friends for their kind liberality in supporting this meeting during its session.

14. Whereas, br. John A. Cornish having tendered his services as Colporteur for this Association on his own resources, the Association, on motion, accepted his services, and the sympathies of this body were extended to him, bidding him God speed to go and do all he can for the cause of Christ.

15. On motion, the Association adjourned to the time and place appointed.　　　　　　AMOS WEAVER. *Moderator*.

AZARIAH WILLIAMS, *Clerk*.

The Bible Society held a meeting on Saturday, August 21st, at 3 oclock.  The Association gave away at this hour ; and after a very interesting address by Elder A. Weaver on the importance of the Bible, the Society proceeded to organize, and elected the following officers for the ensuing year, to wit :  Elder A. Williams, President ; Isaac Kinney, 1st Vice President ;  Isaac A. Park, 2nd Vice President ; Elder Wm. Turner, 3rd Vice President ; Elder Amos Weaver, Secretary and Treasurer.

### LIFE MEMBERS.

Elder Azariah Williams, Isaac A. Park, Alexander Delap and Catharine his wife ; Isaac Kinney, Elder Benjamin Lanier ; Dr. W. H. Wiseman.

*ANNUAL MEMBERS by the payment of fifty cents.*
Wm. Owen, Ebenezer Merrell, Elder A. Weaver, Samuel W. Lanier, Matthias Long, John A. Cornish, Elder Wm. Turner, E. H. Davis, Jesse H. Owen and Michael Redwine.

| | |
|---|---|
| The amount given by Life Members, or a balance, for the past year, | 4 50 |
| Annual Members for this year, | 5 00 |
| Treasurer reported on hand | 32 05 |
| Whole amount paid, | $41 55 |

### TREASURER'S REPORT.

| | |
|---|---|
| Amount received from former Treasurer, br. Avrit, | $16 10 |
| Amount received at the last annual meeting, | 15 95 |
| | $32 05 |

AMOS WEAVER, *Treasurer*.

Elder A. Weaver, and Elder Wm. Turner were appointed to deliver addresses before the B. B. Society at our next annual Association, on Saturda ;　　　　　AZARIAH WILLIAMS *President*.

## A.--Report on Sabbath Schools.

Having examined the letters that were read before this body, we find nothing said concerning these important Schools, to wit the Sabbath School. And we are sorry to see so little interest taken among the Baptists of this Association in regard to Sunday Schools; and we anticipate the beauty and the good that might result in a well organized school at every church in the bounds of this Association. And the Bible says "train up a child in the way he should go, and when he becomes old he will not depart therefrom." We would ask, where is a better place to train a child than at a Sunday School, where he has the Bible to read, and can hear its truths explained when young and tender? We would pray God to give us grace and boldness sufficient to go and build up schools everywhere, believing them to be the accomplishment of much good, in the hands of God. All of which is respectfully submitted: CHAS. TEAGUE, *Chairman.*

## B.--Report on Home and Foreign Missions.

The Committee on Missions submit the following report:

It is a subject in which we should take a deep interest, and to which we are in duty bound to lend a helping hand. The field is white unto the harvest At home and abroad there is much destitution, and it cannot be otherwise than the blood of our fellow-beings will be upon our skirts, if we fold our arms and make no effort to supply the destitute with the gospel of the Son of God. All of which is respectfully submitted. WM. TURNER, *Chairman.*

## C--Report on Bibles, Publications and Periodicals.

The Committee to whom was referred the subject of Bibles, Publications and Periodicals, report that of the Bible, your committee feel that they are unable adequately to speak; it is the book of all books, and should be prized as the dearest treasure on earth. We feel also that we cannot too highly recommend the various publications put forth by our denomination, which shed light on the history, doctrines and usages of the church; the trials and triumphs of eminent saints, &c. We regard also as of great importance that Baptists should be well posted on the movements now making in the religious world, which cannot be done without due attention to our own periodicals. We should especially seek and read such papers as the Biblical Recorder, our own denominational paper, published in Raleigh, by Elder James; the Tennessee Baptist, published in Nashville, Tenn., by J. R. Graves and others, a sterling Baptist paper; the Commission, published in Richmond, Va., by the Secretaries of the Southern Boards for Home and Foreign Missions. Respectfully submitted.

J. A. PARK, *Chairman.*

## D.--Colportage.

Your Committee on Colportage beg leave to report:

We think it a means by which much good may be done. The necessity of distributing Baptist literature through our Association is evidently necessary. It then remains for us to devise the most effectual way of carrying it into effect. There have been many ways tried which have as yet failed to reach the masses of the people. We believe this to be a time when a Colporteur is needed in our midst.— Therefore we recommend this Association to select and countenance a man capable of filling the office of Colporteur. Respectfully submitted.

J. A.

## E.--Report on Temperance.

When we examine the subject of Temperance and take into consideration the different branches of intemperance, we are made to wonder how it is that God's people can be so quiet on that great subject. And especially upon the intemperate use of king alcohol, when we see him making his way to and fro over our country, and leaving behind misery, degradation and death. We are taught in the Word that no drunkard shall see the kingdom of God. And the wise man, Solomon, says: It is as dangerous to use strong drink, as it would be to lie down and sleep in the midst of the sea, or to sleep on the top of a marsh.

Now, brethren, we know that either of these positions would be death. So not having time nor space to discuss the evils of intemperance, we recommend the cause to Baptists. All of which is respectfully submitted.     CHAS. TEAGUE, *Chairman.*

## F.--Report on Baptist State Convention of N. C.

The objects of the convention are to supply destitute places at home and in heathen lands, with the blessed Gospel of Jesus Christ. Also to assist poor young men, who are called of God to preach the Gospel, and are recommended by their churches, in obtaining an education. The convention opens the way by which our donations can be so well applied, and accomplish much good. If 100 persons in each congregation would give ten cents apiece, each church could have one delegate in the Convention; and the sum raised, would be $140, with which much good could be done. And it would be an easy matter to treble that amount, if we had the matter at heart as we should.

Let every member of the Liberty Association not rest contented without doing something in aid of the objects of the Baptist State Convention of North Carolina.

Respectfully submitted.

WM. TURNER, *Chairman.*

## G.--Report on Education.

Your Committee on Education regret very much that their present limits will not allow them the opportunity of entering fully into the merits of so important a subject as the education of the rising generation, and giving a right bias to the mind. We regret very much that christian parents, in this important matter, have manifested too much indifference to the right training of the infant mind; hence our sons and daughters, in the great anxiety to have their education, are sent to Pedo schools, and frequently are placed under teachers that have no piety themselves, and it will take eternity to unfold the evils the church received from this source. And we think it is high time that the church should wake up to meet this evil. Has not many a christian heart been made to bleed from seeing their dear offspring led off in error.

Your Committee, therefore, recommend to every christian parent the proper training of the mind; we further believe that no parent, discharges his or her duty who neglects to give their children a good education as far as their means will afford; and that they should be more eager to bestow or give them a good education, than worldly goods which are often spent to no profit, and the owner left a nuisance to society. Your Committee therefore recommend the patronage of our denominational High Schools, both male and female.

All of which is respectfully submitted.

## H.--Report of Committee on Church Letters, &c.

The Committee on Church Letters and the State of Religion beg leave to submit the following report:

From the statistical information sent up by the churches, there is manifestly an alarming state of things existing in our Association. Coldness seems to prevail throughout its length and breadth. There has been but little or no increase in the last Associational year.

Dear brethren, why is this the case. "God is not slack concerning His promises.' Why then should we thus mourn over our languishing Zion?— The answer is at hand:—The discharge of duty is always accompanied by Heaven's richest blessing.

And, dear brethren, when we are fully aroused to the discharge of duty, God will again visit us, and bless us as in former years. Your committee would earnestly recommend the speedy adoption of some measure by which we may be able to supply the destitute churches and other destitute portions of our Associational bounds with more preaching of the Gospel. We have the means to do much more than we are doing, if we would do what is in our power to do; if we would send our own young ministers to preach to the youths of our destitute portions, and stir up the zeal of our young men who have talents sufficient to make them useful. There would, in the opinion of your committee, in a few years, be such a change as to gladden the heart of every lover of Christ and of man's redemption.

Dear brethren, we have, year after year, written reports on the state of religion, and as often have we complained of our cold condition, and yet we are doing comparatively nothing. There must be a general waking up throughout our bounds. There must be more sacrifice made for the cause of our gracious Redeemer. There must be greater efforts put forth by the lay members of our churches. Your committee would recommend the propriety of a regular weekly prayer meeting in every church and destitute portion of our bounds, as far as possible. There is too much expected of a weak and unsupported ministry.

Dear brethren, in the opinion of your committee, when these things are properly attended to, God will bless us as He is blessing others through the wide domains of our blessed land. All of which is respectfully submitted.

J. H. OWEN, Chairman.

---

**I.** *To the Ministers, Messengers and Delegates composing the Liberty Association, convened at Holloway's M. H., August, 1858.*

DEAR BRETHREN.—We are Baptists, and we love all who love our Lord Jesus Christ; and we desire greatly the peace and harmony of the Church, and that all occasions of hardness among the brethren be taken out of the way. And whereas, Wm. H. H-mner, a former member of the church at Reed's Cross Roads, a brother that we have long known, and whom we still cannot but respect as a christian brother, has been for many years excluded from the fellowship of the Church; and whereas we learn that the difficulties between the said church and him is of such a nature, that they cannot, or have not settled them; and whereas, we know that it would give many good brethren, as well as us, your petitioners, unfeigned gratification to see this difficulty healed, and our brother, Wm. H Hamner, restored to membership among us, and all matters of grievance taken out of the way,—all of which, we believe, could be readily effected if all parties would but go into it in the spirit of Christ.

We therefore affectionately ask your body to advise the church at Reed's Cross Roads, as she is a party to this difficulty, and as such, may not be able to look at all the facts as impartially as she ought, that she submit this whole matter to a council of her brethren, and that this Association advise her to take an early opportunity to invite each church in this Association to send to her assistance on some specified day, a discreet member to be selected by their respective churches, and to commit the settlement of this whole matter into the hands of said brethren when so met; provided, however, that the representatives of not less than a majority of the churches in this Association shall be present in the council. All of which, dear brethren, is affectionately submitted.

BENJAMIN LANIER, ELI COGGIN, FREDERICK BEANBLOOM,
E A. DAVIS, HENRY SMITH, WM OWEN
JAMES ADDERTON, G. F. SMITH, ABRAHAM PALMER.

CPSIA information can be obtained
at www.ICGtesting.com
Printed in the USA
BVHW090727081118
532427BV00011B/405/P